Virtual Clinical Excursions—Maternal Child Nursing

Virtual Clinical Excursions—Maternal Child Nursing

prepared by

Kelly Ann Crum, PhD (ABD), RN
Director, School of Nursing
Associate Professor of Nursing
Maranatha Baptist Bible College
Watertown, Wisconsin

software developed by

Wolfsong Informatics, LLC
Tucson, Arizona

ELSEVIER

ELSEVIER

3251 Riverport Lane
Maryland Heights, Missouri 63043

VIRTUAL CLINICAL EXCURSIONS—MATERNAL CHILD NURSING
Copyright © 2018, Elsevier Inc. All rights reserved.

ISBN: 978-0-323-52394-3

Notice

ISBN: 978-0-323-52394-3

Printed in the United States of America

Last digit is the print number: 9 8 7 6 5 4 3 2 1

Textbooks

**McKinney, James, Murray, Nelson, and Ashwill:
Maternal-Child Nursing, 5th edition**

**Perry, Hockenberry, Lowdermilk, and Wilson:
Maternal Child Nursing Care, 5th edition**

Table of Contents
Virtual Clinical Excursions Workbook

GETTING SET UP WITH VCE ONLINE

The product you have purchased is part of the Evolve Learning System. Please read the following information thoroughly to get started.

■ HOW TO ACCESS YOUR VCE RESOURCES ON EVOLVE

There are two ways to access your VCE Resources on Evolve:

1. If your instructor has enrolled you in your VCE Evolve Resources, you will receive an email with your registration details.

2. If your instructor has asked you to self-enroll in your VCE Evolve Resources, he or she will provide you with your Course ID (for example, 1479_jdoe73_0001). You will then need to follow the instructions at https://evolve.elsevier.com/cs/studentEnroll.html.

■ HOW TO ACCESS THE ONLINE VIRTUAL HOSPITAL

The online virtual hospital is available through the Evolve VCE Resources. There is no software to download or install: the online virtual hospital runs within your Internet browser, using a pop-up window.

■ TECHNICAL REQUIREMENTS

- Broadband connection (DSL or cable)
- 1024 x 768 screen resolution
- Mozilla Firefox 18.0, Internet Explorer 9.0, Google Chrome, or Safari 5 (or higher)
  Note: Pop-up blocking software/settings must be disabled.
- Adobe Acrobat Reader
- Additional technical requirements available at http://evolvesupport.elsevier.com

■ HOW TO ACCESS THE WORKBOOK

There are two ways to access the workbook portion of *Virtual Clinical Excursions:*

1. Print workbook
2. An electronic version of the workbook, available within the VCE Evolve Resources

■ TECHNICAL SUPPORT

Technical support for *Virtual Clinical Excursions* is available by visiting the Technical Support Center at http://evolvesupport.elsevier.com or by calling 1-800-222-9570 inside the United States and Canada.

Trademarks: Windows® and Macintosh® are registered trademarks.

A QUICK TOUR

Welcome to *Virtual Clinical Excursions—Maternal Child Nursing*, a virtual hospital setting in which you can work with multiple complex patient simulations and also learn to access and evaluate the information resources that are essential for high-quality patient care. The virtual hospital, Pacific View Regional Hospital, has realistic architecture and access to patient rooms, a Nurses' Station, and a Medication Room.

◼ BEFORE YOU START

Make sure you have your textbook nearby when you use *Virtual Clinical Excursions*. You will want to consult topic areas in your textbook frequently while working with the virtual hospital and workbook.

◼ HOW TO SIGN IN

- Enter your name in the first section of the sign-in window.
- Next, specify the floor on which you will work by clicking the corresponding button under **Select Floor**. For this quick tour, choose **Obstetrics**.
- Now choose one of the four periods of care in which to work. In Periods of Care 1 through 3, you can actively engage in patient assessment, entry of data in the electronic patient record (EPR), and medication administration. Period of Care 4 presents the day in review. Click the appropriate button under **Select Period of Care**. (For this quick tour, choose **Period of Care 1: 0730-0815**.)
- Click **Start**. This takes you to the Patient List screen (see the *How to Select a Patient* section below). Note that the virtual time is provided in the box at the lower left corner of the screen (0730, because we chose Period of Care 1).

Note: If you choose to work during Period of Care 4: 1900-2000, the Patient List screen is skipped because you are not able to visit patients or administer medications during the shift. Instead, you are taken directly to the Nurses' Station, where the records of all the patients on the floor are available for your review.

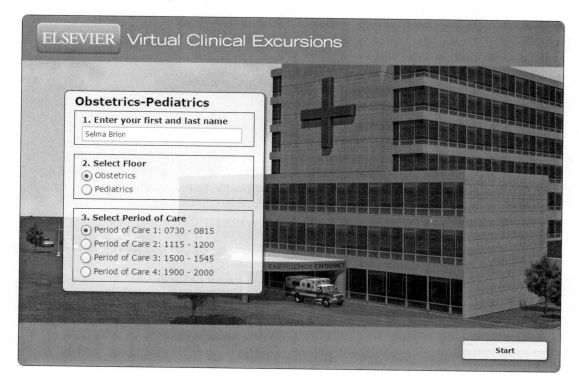

■ PATIENT LIST

OBSTETRICS UNIT

Dorothy Grant (Room 201)
30-week intrauterine pregnancy—A 25-year-old multipara Caucasian female admitted with abdominal trauma following a domestic violence incident. Her complications include preterm labor and extensive social issues such as acquiring safe housing for her family upon discharge.

Stacey Crider (Room 202)
27-week intrauterine pregnancy—A 21-year-old primigravida Native American female admitted for intravenous tocolysis, bacterial vaginosis, and poorly controlled insulin-dependent gestational diabetes. Strained family relationships and social isolation complicate this patient's ability to comply with strict dietary requirements and prenatal care.

Kelly Brady (Room 203)
26-week intrauterine pregnancy—A 35-year-old primigravida Caucasian female urgently admitted for progressive symptoms of preeclampsia. A history of inadequate coping with major life stressors leave her at risk for a recurrence of depression as she faces a diagnosis of HELLP syndrome and the delivery of a severely premature infant.

Maggie Gardner (Room 204)
22-week intrauterine pregnancy—A 41-year-old multigravida African-American female admitted for a high-risk pregnancy evaluation and rule out diagnosis of systemic lupus erythematosus. Coping with chronic pain, fatigue, and a history of multiple miscarriages contribute to an anxiety disorder and the need for social service intervention.

Gabriela Valenzuela (Room 205)
34-week intrauterine pregnancy—A 21-year-old primigravida Hispanic female with a history of mitral valve prolapse admitted for uterine cramping and vaginal bleeding suggestive of placental abruption following an unrestrained motor vehicle accident. Her needs include staff support for an unprepared-for labor and possible preterm birth.

Laura Wilson (Room 206)
37-week intrauterine pregnancy—An 18-year-old primigravida Caucasian female urgently admitted after being found unconscious at home. Her complications include HIV-positive status and chronic polysubstance abuse. Unrealistic expectations of parenthood and living with a chronic illness combined with strained family relations prompt comprehensive social and psychiatric evaluations initiated on the day of simulation.

PEDIATRICS UNIT

George Gonzalez (Room 301)
Diabetic ketoacidosis—An 11-year-old Hispanic male admitted for stabilization of blood glucose level and diabetic re-education associated with his diagnosis of type 1 diabetes mellitus. This patient's poor compliance with insulin therapy and dietary regime have resulted in frequent and repeated hospital admissions for diabetic ketoacidosis.

Tommy Douglas (Room 302)
Traumatic brain injury—A 6-year-old Caucasian male transferred from the Pediatric Intensive Care Unit in preparation for organ donation. This patient is status post ventriculostomy with negative intracerebral blood flow and requires extensive hemodynamic monitoring and support, along with compassionate family care.

Carrie Richards (Room 303)
Bronchiolitis—A 3½-month-old African-American female admitted with respiratory distress due to respiratory syncytial virus, along with dehydration and an inadequate nutritional status. Parent education and support are among her primary needs.

Stephanie Brown (Room 304)

Meningitis—A 3-year-old African-American female with a history of spastic cerebral palsy admitted for intravenous antibiotic therapy, neurologic monitoring, and support for a diagnosis of acute meningitis. Maintenance of physical and occupational programs addressing her mobility limitations complicate her acute care stay.

Tiffany Sheldon (Room 305)

Anorexia nervosa—A 14-year-old Caucasian female admitted for dehydration, electrolyte imbalance, and malnutrition following a syncope episode at home. This patient has a history of eating disorders, which have resulted in multiple hospital admissions and strained family dynamics between mother and daughter.

■ HOW TO SELECT A PATIENT

- You can choose one or more patients to work with from the Patient List by checking the box to the left of the patient name(s). For this quick tour, select Dorothy Grant. (In order to receive a scorecard for a patient, the patient must be selected before proceeding to the Nurses' Station.)
- Click on **Get Report** to the right of the medical records number (MRN) to view a summary of the patient's care during the 12-hour period before your arrival on the unit.
- After reviewing the report, click on **Go to Nurses' Station** in the right lower corner to begin your care. (*Note:* If you have been assigned to care for multiple patients, you can click on **Return to Patient List** to select and review the report for each additional patient before going to the Nurses' Station.)

Note: Even though the Patient List is initially skipped when you sign in to work for Period of Care 4, you can still access this screen if you wish to review the shift report for any of the patients. To do so, simply click on **Patient List** near the top left corner of the Nurses' Station (or click on the clipboard to the left of the Kardex). Then click on **Get Report** for the patient(s) whose care you are reviewing. This may be done during any period of care.

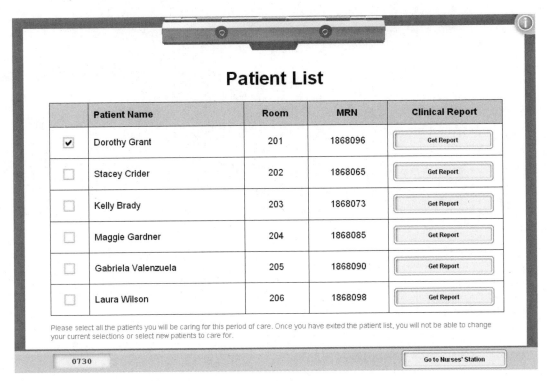

Patient List

	Patient Name	Room	MRN	Clinical Report
☑	Dorothy Grant	201	1868096	Get Report
☐	Stacey Crider	202	1868065	Get Report
☐	Kelly Brady	203	1868073	Get Report
☐	Maggie Gardner	204	1868085	Get Report
☐	Gabriela Valenzuela	205	1868090	Get Report
☐	Laura Wilson	206	1868098	Get Report

Please select all the patients you will be caring for this period of care. Once you have exited the patient list, you will not be able to change your current selections or select new patients to care for.

0730

Go to Nurses' Station

■ **HOW TO FIND A PATIENT'S RECORDS**

NURSES' STATION

Within the Nurses' Station, you will see:

1. A clipboard that contains the patient list for that floor.
2. A chart rack with patient charts labeled by room number, a notebook labeled Kardex, and a notebook labeled MAR (Medication Administration Record).
3. A desktop computer with access to the Electronic Patient Record (EPR).
4. A tool bar across the top of the screen that can also be used to access the Patient List, EPR, Chart, MAR, and Kardex. This tool bar is also accessible from each patient's room.
5. A Drug Guide containing information about the medications you are able to administer to your patients.
6. A Laboratory Guide containing normal value ranges for all laboratory tests you may come across in the virtual patient hospital.
7. A tool bar across the bottom of the screen that can be used to access the Floor Map, patient rooms, Medication Room, and Drug Guide.

As you run your cursor over an item, it will be highlighted. To select, simply click on the item. As you use these resources, you will always be able to return to the Nurses' Station by clicking on the **Return to Nurses' Station** bar located in the right lower corner of your screen.

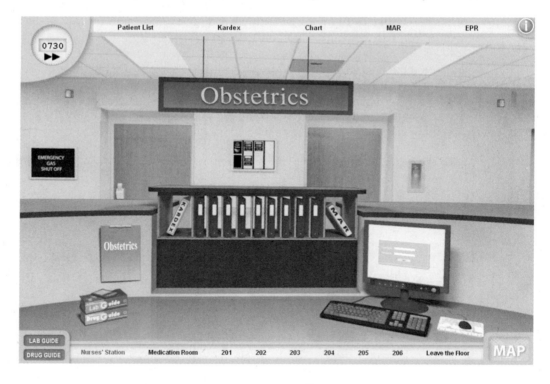

MEDICATION ADMINISTRATION RECORD (MAR)

The MAR icon located on the tool bar at the top of your screen accesses current 24-hour medications for each patient. Click on the icon and the MAR will open. (*Note:* You can also access the MAR by clicking on the MAR notebook on the far right side of the book rack in the center of the screen.) Within the MAR, tabs on the right side of the screen allow you to select patients by room number. Be careful to make sure you select the correct tab number for *your* patient rather than simply reading the first record that appears after the MAR opens. Each MAR sheet lists the following:

- Medications
- Route and dosage of each medication
- Times of administration of each medication

Note: The MAR changes each day. Expired MARs are stored in the patients' charts.

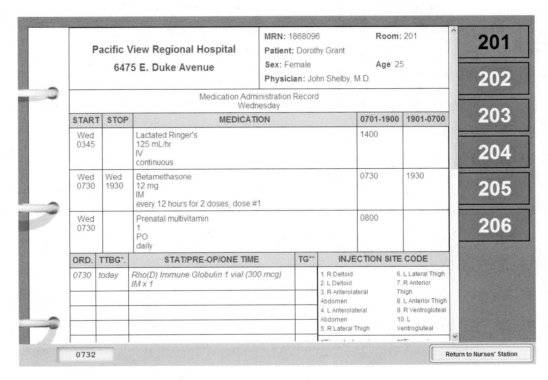

CHARTS

To access patient charts, either click on the **Chart** icon at the top of your screen or anywhere within the chart rack in the center of the Nurses' Station screen. When the close-up view appears, the individual charts are labeled by room number. To open a chart, click on the room number of the patient whose chart you wish to review. The patient's name and allergies will appear on the left side of the screen, along with a list of tabs on the right side of the screen, allowing you to view the following data:

- Allergies
- Physician's Orders
- Physician's Notes
- Nurse's Notes
- Laboratory Reports
- Diagnostic Reports
- Surgical Reports
- Consultations

- Patient Education
- History and Physical
- Nursing Admission
- Expired MARs
- Consents
- Mental Health
- Admissions
- Emergency Department

Information appears in real time. The entries are in reverse chronologic order, so use the down arrow at the right side of each chart page to scroll down to view previous entries. Flip from tab to tab to view multiple data fields or click on **Return to Nurses' Station** in the lower right corner of the screen to exit the chart.

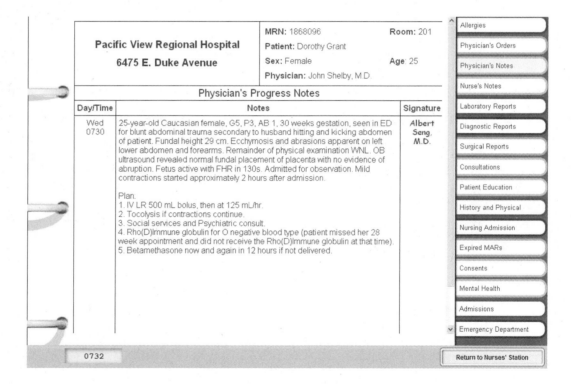

ELECTRONIC PATIENT RECORD (EPR)

The EPR can be accessed from the computer in the Nurses' Station or from the EPR icon located in the tool bar at the top of your screen. To access a patient's EPR:
- Click on either the computer screen or the **EPR** icon.
- Your username and password are automatically filled in.
- Click on **Login** to enter the EPR.
- *Note:* Like the MAR, the EPR is arranged numerically. Thus when you enter, you are initially shown the records of the patient in the lowest room number on the floor. To view the correct data for *your* patient, remember to select the correct room number, using the drop-down menu for the Patient field at the top left corner of the screen.

The EPR used in Pacific View Regional Hospital represents a composite of commercial versions being used in hospitals. You can access the EPR:
- to review existing data for a patient (by room number).
- to enter data you collect while working with a patient.

The EPR is updated daily, so no matter what day or part of a shift you are working, there will be a current EPR with the patient's data from the past days of the current hospital stay. This type of simulated EPR allows you to examine how data for different attributes have changed over time, as well as to examine data for all of a patient's attributes at a particular time. The EPR is fully functional (as it is in a real-life hospital). You can enter such data as blood pressure, breath sounds, and certain treatments. The EPR will not, however, allow you to enter data for a previous time period. Use the arrows at the bottom of the screen to move forward and backward in time.

Patient Room: 201 ▾	Category: Vital Signs ▾			Electronic Patient Records
Name: Dorothy Grant	**Wed 0700**	**Wed 0715**	**Wed 0730**	**Code Meanings**
PAIN: LOCATION	A			
PAIN: RATING	1-2			
PAIN: CHARACTERISTICS	I			
PAIN: VOCAL CUES				
PAIN: FACIAL CUES				
PAIN: BODILY CUESS				
PAIN: SYSTEM CUES				
PAIN: FUNCTIONAL EFFECTS				
PAIN: PREDISPOSING FACTORS				
PAIN: RELIEVING FACTORS				
PCA				
TEMPERATURE (F)	98.2			
TEMPERATURE (C)				
MODE OF MEASUREMENT	O			
SYSTOLIC PRESSURE	126			
DIASTOLIC PRESSURE	68			
BP MODE OF MEASUREMENT	NIBP			
HEART RATE	70			
RESPIRATORY RATE	18			
SpO2 (%)	96			
BLOOD GLUCOSE				
WEIGHT				
HEIGHT				

| 0730 | | Return to Nurses' Station |

At the top of the EPR screen, you can choose patients by their room numbers. In addition, you have access to 17 different categories of patient data. To change patients or data categories, click the down arrow to the right of the room number or category.

The categories of patient data in the EPR are as follows:

- Vital Signs
- Respiratory
- Cardiovascular
- Neurologic
- Gastrointestinal
- Excretory
- Musculoskeletal
- Integumentary
- Reproductive
- Psychosocial
- Wounds and Drains
- Activity
- Hygiene and Comfort
- Safety
- Nutrition
- IV
- Intake and Output

Remember, each hospital selects its own codes. The codes used in the EPR at Pacific View Regional Hospital may be different from ones you have seen in your clinical rotations. Take some time to acquaint yourself with the codes. Within the Vital Signs category, click on any item in the left column (e.g., Pain: Characteristics). In the far-right column, you will see a list of code meanings for the possible findings and/or descriptors for that assessment area.

You will use the codes to record the data you collect as you work with patients. Click on the box in the last time column to the right of any item and wait for the code meanings applicable to that entry to appear. Select the appropriate code to describe your assessment findings and type it in the box. (*Note:* If no cursor appears within the box, click on the box again until the blue shading disappears and the blinking cursor appears.) Once the data are typed in this box, they are entered into the patient's record for this period of care only.

To leave the EPR, click on **Exit EPR** in the bottom right corner of the screen.

■ VISITING A PATIENT

From the Nurses' Station, click on the room number of the patient you wish to visit (in the tool bar at the bottom of your screen). Once you are inside the room, you will see a still photo of your patient in the top left corner. To verify that this is the correct patient, click on the **Check Armband** icon to the right of the photo. The patient's identification data will appear. If you click on **Check Allergies** (the next icon to the right), a list of the patient's allergies (if any) will replace the photo.

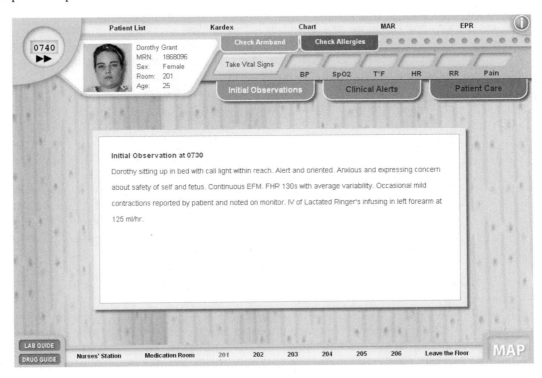

Also located in the patient's room are multiple icons you can use to assess the patient or the patient's medications. A virtual clock is provided in the upper left corner of the room to monitor your progress in real time. (*Note:* The fast-forward icon within the virtual clock will advance the time by 2-minute intervals when clicked.)

- The tool bar across the top of the screen allows you to check the **Patient List**, access the **EPR** to check or enter data, and view the patient's **Chart**, **MAR**, or **Kardex**.

- The **Take Vital Signs** icon allows you to measure the patient's up-to-the-minute blood pressure, oxygen saturation, temperature, heart rate, respiratory rate, and pain level.

- Each time you enter a patient's room, you are given an Initial Observation report to review (in the text box under the patient's photo). These notes are provided to give you a "look" at the patient as if you had just stepped into the room. You can also click on the **Initial Observations** icon to return to this box from other views within the patient's room. To the right of this icon is **Clinical Alerts**, a resource that allows you to make decisions about priority medication interventions based on emerging data collected in real time. Check this screen throughout your period of care to avoid missing critical information related to recently ordered or STAT medications.

- Clicking on **Patient Care** opens up three specific learning environments within the patient room: **Physical Assessment**, **Nurse-Client Interactions**, and **Medication Administration**.

- To perform a **Physical Assessment**, choose a body area (such as **Head & Neck**) from the column of yellow buttons. This activates a list of system subcategories for that body area (e.g., see **Sensory**, **Neurologic**, etc. in the green boxes). After you select the system you wish to evaluate, a brief description of the assessment findings will appear in a box to the right. A still photo provides a "snapshot" of how an assessment of this area might be done or what the finding might look like. For every body area, you can also click on **Equipment** on the right side of the screen.

- To the right of the Physical Assessment icon is **Nurse-Client Interactions**. Clicking on this icon will reveal the times and titles of any videos available for viewing. (*Note:* If the video you wish to see is not listed, this means you have not yet reached the correct virtual time to view that video. Check the virtual clock; you may return to access the video once its designated time has occurred—as long as you do so within the same period of care. Or you can click on the fast-forward icon within the virtual clock to advance the time by 2-minute intervals. You will then need to click again on **Patient Care** and **Nurse-Client Interactions** to refresh the screen.) To view a listed video, click on the white arrow to the right of the video title. Use the control buttons below the video to start, stop, pause, rewind, or fast-forward the action or to mute the sound.

- **Medication Administration** is the pathway that allows you to review and administer medications to a patient after you have prepared them in the Medication Room. This process is also addressed further in the *How to Prepare Medications* section below and in *Medications* in **A Detailed Tour**. For additional hands-on practice, see *Reducing Medication Errors* below **A Quick Tour** and **A Detailed Tour** in your resources.

■ HOW TO CHANGE PATIENTS OR CHANGE PERIODS OF CARE

How to Change Patients or Periods of Care: To change patients, simply click on the new patient's room number. (You cannot receive a scorecard for a new patient, however, unless you have already selected that patient on the Patient List screen.) To change to a new period of care or to restart the virtual clock, click on **Leave the Floor** and then on **Restart the Program**.

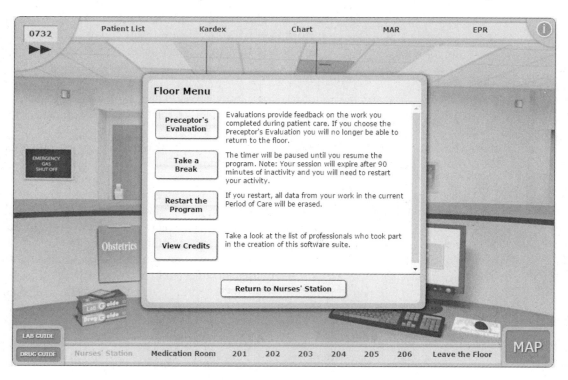

■ HOW TO PREPARE MEDICATIONS

From the Nurses' Station or the patient's room, you can access the Medication Room by clicking on the icon in the tool bar at the bottom of your screen to the left of the patient room numbers.

In the Medication Room you have access to the following (from left to right):

- A preparation area is located on the counter under the cabinets. To begin the medication preparation process, click on the tray on the counter or click on the **Preparation** icon at the top of the screen. The next screen leads you through a specific sequence (called the Preparation Wizard) to prepare medications one at a time for administration to a patient. However, no medication has been selected at this time. We will do this while working with a patient in **A Detailed Tour**. To exit this screen, click on **View Medication Room**.

- To the right of the cabinets (and above the refrigerator), IV storage bins are provided. Click on the bins themselves or on the **IV Storage** icon at the top of the screen. The bins are labeled **Microinfusion**, **Small Volume**, and **Large Volume**. Click on an individual bin to see a list of its contents. If you needed to prepare an IV medication at this time, you could click on the medication and its label would appear to the right under the patient's name. (*Note:* You can **Open** and **Close** any medication label by clicking the appropriate icon.) Next, you would click **Put Medication on Tray**. If you ever change your mind or decide that you have put the incorrect medication on the tray, you can reverse your actions by highlighting the medication on the tray and then clicking **Put Medication in Bin**. Click **Close Bin** in the right bottom corner to exit. **View Medication Room** brings you back to a full view of the entire room.

- A refrigerator is located under the IV storage bins to hold any medications that must be stored below room temperature. Click on the refrigerator door or on the **Refrigerator** icon at the top of the screen. Then click on the close-up view of the door to access the medications. When you are finished, click **Close Door** and then **View Medication Room**.

- To prepare controlled substances, click the **Automated System** icon at the top of the screen or click the computer monitor located to the right of the IV storage bins. A login screen will appear; your name and password are automatically filled in. Click **Login**. Select the patient for whom you wish to access medications; then select the correct medication drawer to open (they are stored alphabetically). Click **Open Drawer**, highlight the proper medication, and choose **Put Medication on Tray**. When you are finished, click **Close Drawer** and then **View Medication Room**.

- Next to the Automated System is a set of drawers identified by patient room number. To access these, click on the drawers or on the **Unit Dosage** icon at the top of the screen. This provides a close-up view of the drawers. To open a drawer, click on the room number of the patient you are working with. Next, click on the medication you would like to prepare for the patient, and a label will appear, listing the medication strength, units, and dosage per unit. To exit, click **Close Drawer**; then click **View Medication Room**.

At any time, you can learn about a medication you wish to prepare for a patient by clicking on the **Drug** icon in the bottom left corner of the medication room screen or by clicking the **Drug Guide** book on the counter to the right of the unit dosage drawers. The **Drug Guide** provides information about the medications commonly included in nursing drug handbooks. Nutritional supplements and maintenance intravenous fluid preparations are not included. Highlight a medication in the alphabetical list; relevant information about the drug will appear in the screen below. To exit, click **Return to Medication Room**.

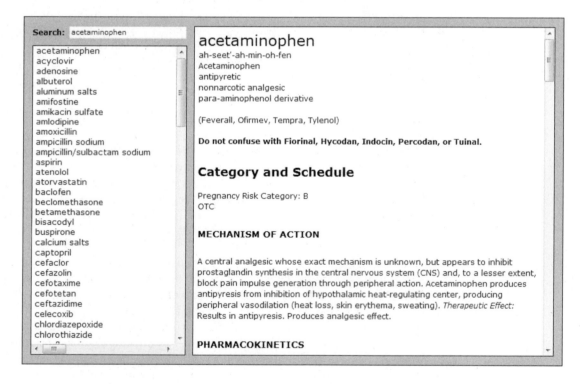

To access the MAR from the Medication Room and to review the medications ordered for a patient, click on the **MAR** icon located in the tool bar at the top of your screen and then click on the correct tab for your patient's room number. You may also click the **Review MAR** icon in the tool bar at the bottom of your screen from inside each medication storage area.

After you have chosen and prepared medications, go to the patient's room to administer them by clicking on the room number in the bottom tool bar. Inside the patient's room, click **Patient Care** and then **Medication Administration** and follow the proper administration sequence.

■ PRECEPTOR'S EVALUATIONS

When you have finished a session, click on **Leave the Floor** to go to the Floor Menu. At this point, you can click on the top icon (**Preceptor's Evaluation**) to receive a scorecard that provides feedback on the work you completed during patient care.

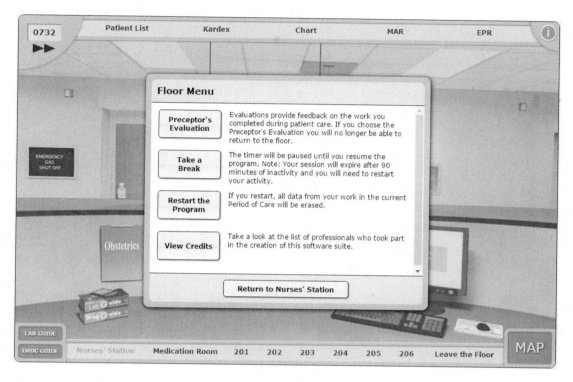

Evaluations are available for each patient you selected when you signed in for the current period of care. Click on the **Medication Scorecard** icon to see an example.

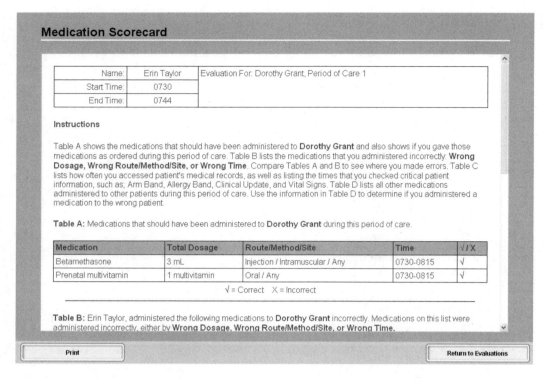

The scorecard compares the medications you administered to a patient during a period of care with what should have been administered. Table A lists the correct medications. Table B lists any medications that were administered incorrectly.

Remember, not every medication listed on the MAR should necessarily be given. For example, a patient might have an allergy to a drug that was ordered, or a medication might have been improperly transcribed to the MAR. Predetermined medication "errors" embedded within the program challenge you to exercise critical thinking skills and professional judgment when deciding to administer a medication, just as you would in a real hospital. Use all your available resources, such as the patient's chart and the MAR, to make your decision.

Table C lists the resources that were available to assist you in medication administration. It also documents whether and when you accessed these resources. For example, did you check the patient armband or perform a check of vital signs? If so, when?

You can click **Print** to get a copy of this report if needed. When you have finished reviewing the scorecard, click **Return to Evaluations** and then **Return to Menu**.

■ FLOOR MAP

To get a general sense of your location within the hospital, you can click on the **Map** icon found in the lower right corner of most of the screens in the *Virtual Clinical Excursions—Maternal Child Nursing* program. (*Note:* If you are following this quick tour step by step, you will need to **Restart the Program** from the Floor Menu, sign in again, and go to the Nurses' Station to access the map.) When you click the **Map** icon, a floor map appears, showing the layout of the floor you are currently on, as well as a directory of the patients and services on that floor. As you move your cursor over the directory list, the location of each room is highlighted on the map (and vice versa). The floor map can be accessed from the Nurses' Station, Medication Room, and each patient's room.

A DETAILED TOUR

If you wish to more thoroughly understand the capabilities of *Virtual Clinical Excursions—Maternal Child Nursing*, take a detailed tour by completing the following section. During this tour, we will work with a specific patient to introduce you to all the different components and learning opportunities available within the software.

■ WORKING WITH A PATIENT

Sign in to work on the Obstetrics Floor for Period of Care 1 (0730-0815). From the Patient List, select Dorothy Grant in Room 201; however, do not go to the Nurses' Station yet.

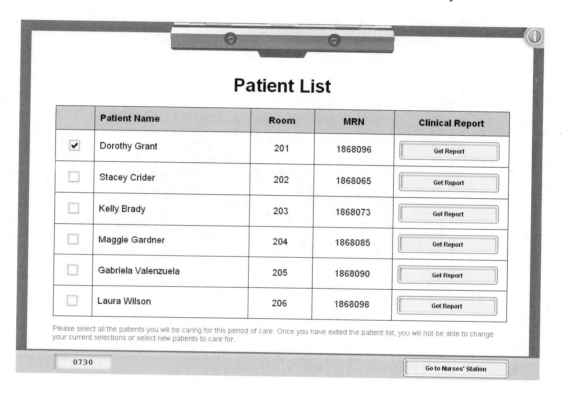

■ REPORT

In hospitals, when one shift ends and another begins, the outgoing nurse who attended a patient will give a verbal and sometimes a written summary of that patient's condition to the incoming nurse who will assume care for the patient. This summary is called a report and is an important source of data to provide an overview of a patient. Your first task is to get the clinical report on Dorothy Grant. To do this, click **Get Report** in the far right column in this patient's row. From a brief review of this summary, identify the problems and areas of concern that you will need to address for this patient.

When you have finished noting any areas of concern, click **Go to Nurses' Station**.

■ CHARTS

You can access Dorothy Grant's chart from the Nurses' Station or from the patient's room (201). From the Nurses' Station, click on the chart rack or on the **Chart** icon in the tool bar at the top of your screen. Next, click on the chart labeled **201** to open the medical record for Dorothy Grant. Click on the **Emergency Department** tab to view a record of why this patient was admitted.

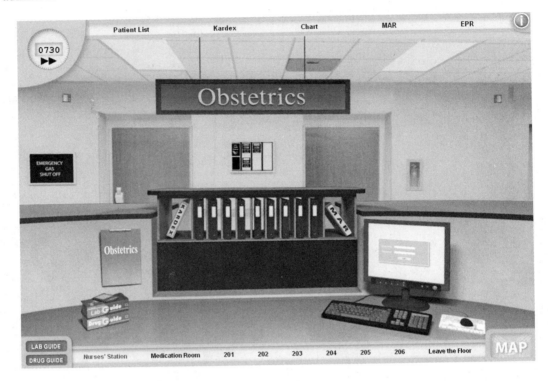

How many days has Dorothy Grant been in the hospital?

What tests were done upon her arrival in the Emergency Department and why?

What was the reason for her admission?

You should also click on **Diagnostic Reports** to learn what additional tests or procedures were performed and when. Finally, review the **Nursing Admission** and **History and Physical** to learn about the health history of this patient. When you are done reviewing the chart, click **Return to Nurses' Station**.

■ MEDICATIONS

Open the Medication Administration Record (MAR) by clicking on the **MAR** icon in the tool bar at the top of your screen. *Remember:* The MAR automatically opens to the first occupied room number on the floor—which is not necessarily your patient's room number! Because you need to access Dorothy Grant's MAR, click on tab **201** (her room number). Always make sure you are giving the *Right Drug to the Right Patient!*

Examine the list of medications ordered for Dorothy Grant. In the table below, list the medications that need to be given during this period of care (0730-0815). For each medication, note the dosage, route, and time to be given.

Time	Medication	Dosage	Route

Click on **Return to Nurses' Station**. Next, click on **201** on the bottom tool bar and then verify that you are indeed in Dorothy Grant's room. Select **Clinical Alerts** (the icon to the right of Initial Observations) to check for any emerging data that might affect your medication administration priorities. Next, go to the patient's chart (click on the **Chart** icon; then click on **201**). When the chart opens, select the **Physician's Orders** tab.

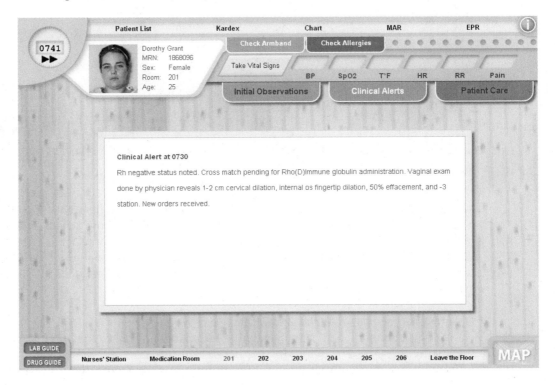

Review the orders. Have any new medications been ordered? Return to the MAR (click **Return to Room 201**; then click **MAR**). Verify that any new medications have been correctly transcribed to the MAR. Mistakes are sometimes made in the transcription process in the hospital setting, and it is sound practice to double-check any new order.

Are there any patient assessments you will need to perform before administering these medications? If so, return to Room 201 and click on **Patient Care** and then **Physical Assessment** to complete those assessments before proceeding.

Now click on the **Medication Room** icon in the tool bar at the bottom of your screen to locate and prepare the medications for Dorothy Grant.

In the Medication Room, you must access the medications for Dorothy Grant from the specific dispensing system in which each medication is stored. Locate each medication that needs to be given in this time period and click on **Put Medication on Tray** as appropriate. (*Hint:* Look in **Unit Dosage** drawer first.) When you are finished, click on **Close Drawer** and then on **View Medication Room**. Now click on the medication tray on the counter on the left side of the medication room screen to begin preparing the medications you have selected. (*Remember:* You can also click **Preparation** in the tool bar at the top of screen.)

In the preparation area, you should see a list of the medications you put on the tray in the previous steps. Click on the first medication and then click **Prepare**. Follow the onscreen instructions of the Preparation Wizard, providing any data requested. As an example, let's follow the preparation process for betamethasone, one of the medications due to be administered to Dorothy Grant during this period of care. To begin, click on **Betamethasone**; then click **Prepare**. Now work through the Preparation Wizard sequence as detailed below:

> Amount of medication in the ampule: 5 mL.
> Enter the amount of medication you will draw up into a syringe: <u>**3**</u> mL.
> Click **Next**.
> Select the patient you wish to set aside the medication for: **Room 201, Dorothy Grant**.
> Click **Finish**.
> Click **Return to Medication Room**.

Follow this same basic process for the other medications due to be administered to Dorothy Grant during this period of care. (*Hint:* Look in **IV Storage** and **Automated System**.)

PREPARATION WIZARD EXCEPTIONS

- Some medications in *Virtual Clinical Excursions—Maternal Child Nursing* are prepared by the pharmacy (e.g., IV antibiotics) and taken to the patient room as a whole. This is common practice in most hospitals.
- Blood products are not administered by students through the *Virtual Clinical Excursions—Maternal Child Nursing* simulations because blood administration follows specific protocols not covered in this program.
- The *Virtual Clinical Excursions—Maternal Child Nursing* simulations do not allow for mixing more than one type of medication, such as regular and Lente insulins, in the same syringe. In the clinical setting, when multiple types of insulin are ordered for a patient, the regular insulin is drawn up first, followed by the longer-acting insulin. Insulin is always administered in a special unit-marked syringe.

Now return to Room 201 (click on **201** on the bottom tool bar) to administer Dorothy Grant's medications.

At any time during the medication administration process, you can perform a further review of systems, take vital signs, check information contained within the chart, or verify patient identity and allergies. Inside Dorothy Grant's room, click **Take Vital Signs**. (*Note:* These findings change over time to reflect the temporal changes you would find in a patient similar to Dorothy Grant.)

When you have gathered all the data you need, click on **Patient Care** and then select **Medication Administration**. Any medications you prepared in the previous steps should be listed on the left side of your screen. Let's continue the administration process with the betamethasone ordered for Dorothy Grant. Click to highlight **Betamethasone** in the list of medications. Next, click on the down arrow to the right of **Select** and choose **Administer** from the drop-down menu. This will activate the Administration Wizard. Complete the Wizard sequence as follows:

- Route: **Injection**
- Method: **Intramuscular**
- Site: **Any**
- Click **Administer to Patient** arrow.
- Would you like to document this administration in the MAR? **Yes**
- Click **Finish** arrow.

Your selections are recorded by a tracking system and evaluated on a Medication Scorecard stored under Preceptor's Evaluations. This scorecard can be viewed, printed, and given to your instructor. To access the Preceptor's Evaluations, click on **Leave the Floor**. When the Floor Menu appears, select **Look at Your Preceptor's Evaluation**. Then click on **Medication Scorecard** inside the box with Dorothy Grant's name (see example on the following page).

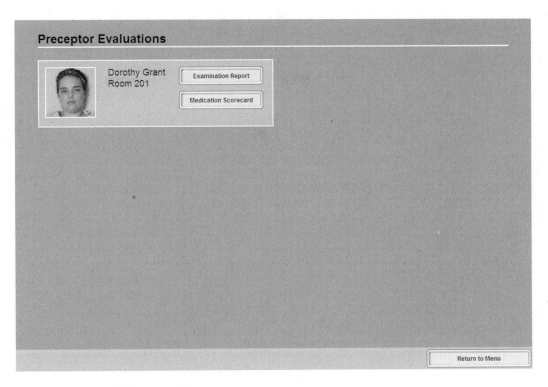

■ MEDICATION SCORECARD

- First, review Table A. Was betamethasone given correctly? Did you give the other medications as ordered?
- Table B shows you which (if any) medications you gave incorrectly.
- Table C addresses the resources used for Dorothy Grant. Did you access the patient's chart, MAR, EPR, or Kardex as needed to make safe medication administration decisions?
- Did you check the patient's armband to verify her identity? Did you check whether your patient had any known allergies to medications? Were vital signs taken?

When you have finished reviewing the scorecard, click **Return to Evaluations** and then **Return to Menu**.

■ VITAL SIGNS

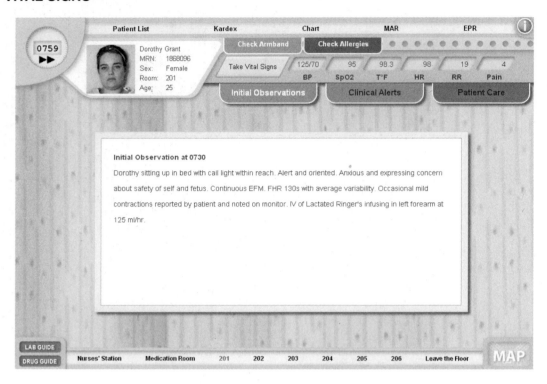

Vital signs, often considered the traditional "signs of life," include body temperature, heart rate, respiratory rate, blood pressure, oxygen saturation of the blood, and pain level.

Inside Dorothy Grant's room, click **Take Vital Signs**. (*Note:* If you are following this detailed tour step by step, you will need to **Restart the Program** from the Floor Menu, sign in again for Period of Care 1, and navigate to Room 201.) Collect vital signs for this patient and record them below. Note the time at which you collected each of these data. (*Remember:* You can take vital signs at any time. The data change over time to reflect the temporal changes you would find in a patient similar to Dorothy Grant.)

Vital Signs	Findings/Time
Blood pressure	
O$_2$ saturation	
Temperature	
Heart rate	
Respiratory rate	
Pain rating	

After you are done, click on the **EPR** icon located in the tool bar at the top of the screen. Your username and password are automatically provided. Click on **Login** to enter the EPR. To access Dorothy Grant's records, click on the down arrow next to Patient and choose her room number, **201**. Select **Vital Signs** as the category. Next, in the empty time column on the far right, record the vital signs data you just collected in the patient's room. If you need help with this process, refer to the Electronic Patient Record (EPR) section of the Quick Tour. Now compare these findings with the data you collected earlier for this patient's vital signs. Use these earlier findings to establish a baseline for each of the vital signs.

a. Are any of the data you collected significantly different from the baseline for a particular vital sign?

Circle One: Yes   No

b. If "Yes," which data are different?

■ PHYSICAL ASSESSMENT

After you have finished examining the EPR for vital signs, click **Exit EPR** to return to Room 201. Click **Patient Care** and then **Physical Assessment**. Think about the information you received in the report at the beginning of this shift, as well as what you may have learned about this patient from the chart. Based on this, what area(s) of examination should you pay most attention to at this time? Is there any equipment you should be monitoring? Conduct a physical assessment of the body areas and systems that you consider priorities for Dorothy Grant. For example, select **Head & Neck**; then click on and assess **Sensory** and **Lymphatic**. Complete any other assessment(s) you think are necessary at this time. In the following table, record the data you collected during this examination.

Area of Examination	Findings
Head & Neck Sensory	
Head & Neck Lymphatic	

After you have finished collecting these data, return to the EPR. Compare the data that were already in the record with those you just collected.

a.   Are any of the data you collected significantly different from the baselines for this patient?

Circle One: Yes   No

b.   If "Yes," which data are different?

■ NURSE-CLIENT INTERACTIONS

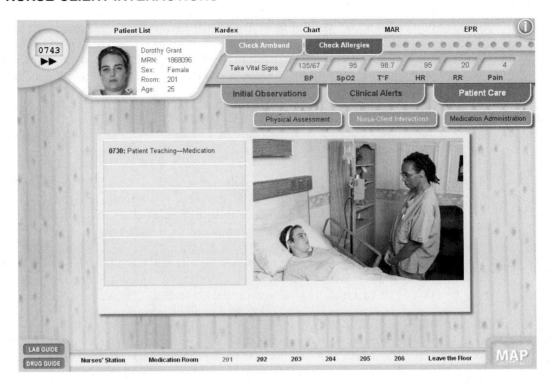

Click on **Patient Care** from inside Dorothy Grant's room (201). Now click on **Nurse-Client Interactions** to access a short video titled **Patient Teaching—Medication**, which is available for viewing at or after 0730 (based on the virtual clock in the upper left corner of your screen; see *Note* below). To begin the video, click on the white arrow next to its title. You will observe a nurse communicating with Dorothy Grant. There are many variations of nursing practice, some exemplifying "best" practice and some not. Note whether the nurse in this interaction displays professional behavior and compassionate care. Are her words congruent with what is going on with the patient? Does this interaction "feel right" to you? If not, how would you handle this situation differently? Explain.

Note: If the video you wish to view is not listed, this means you have not yet reached the correct virtual time to view that video. Check the virtual clock; you may return to access the video once its designated time has occurred—as long as you do so within the same period of care. Or you can click on the fast-forward icon within the virtual clock to advance the time by 2-minute intervals. You will then need to click again on **Patient Care** and **Nurse-Client Interactions** to refresh the screen.

At least one Nurse-Client Interactions video is available during each period of care. Viewing these videos can help you learn more about what is occurring with a patient at a certain time and also prompt you to discern between nurse communications that are ideal and those that need improvement. Compassionate care and the ability to communicate clearly are essential components of delivering quality nursing care, and it is during your clinical time that you will begin to refine these skills.

■ COLLECTING AND EVALUATING DATA

Each of the activities you perform in the Patient Care environment generates a significant amount of assessment data. Remember that after you collect data, you can record your findings in the EPR. You can also review the EPR, patient's chart, videos, and MAR at any time. You will get plenty of practice collecting and then evaluating data in context of the patient's course.

Now, here's an important question for you:

> Did the previous sequence of exercises provide the most efficient way to assess Dorothy Grant?

For example, you went to the patient's room to get vital signs, then back to the EPR to enter data and compare your findings with extant data. Next, you went back to the patient's room to do a physical examination, then again back to the EPR to enter and review data. If this back-and-forth process of data collection and recording seemed inefficient, remember the following:

- Plan all of your nursing activities to maximize efficiency, while at the same time optimizing the quality of patient care. (Think about what data you might need before performing certain tasks. For example, do you need to check a heart rate before administering a cardiac medication or check an IV site before starting an infusion?)

- You collect a tremendous amount of data when you work with a patient. Very few people can accurately remember all these data for more than a few minutes. Develop efficient assessment skills, and record data as soon as possible after collecting them.

- Assessment data are only the starting point for the nursing process.

Make a clear distinction between these first exercises and how you actually provide nursing care. These initial exercises were designed to involve you actively in the use of different software components. This workbook focuses on sensible practices for implementing the nursing process in ways that ensure the highest-quality care of patients.

Most important, remember that a human being changes through time, and that these changes include both the physical and psychosocial facets of a person as a living organism. Think about this for a moment. Some patients may change physically in a very short time (a patient with emerging myocardial infarction) or more slowly (a patient with a chronic illness). Patients' overall physical and psychosocial conditions may improve or deteriorate. They may have effective coping skills and familial support, or they may feel alone and full of despair. In fact, each individual is a complex mix of physical and psychosocial elements, and at least some of these elements usually change through time.

Thus it is crucial that you *DO NOT* think of the nursing process as a simple one-time, five-step procedure consisting of assessment, nursing diagnosis, planning, implementation, and evaluation. Rather, the nursing process should be utilized as a creative and systematic approach to delivering nursing care. Furthermore, because all living organisms are constantly changing, we must apply the nursing process over and over. Each time we follow the nursing process for an individual patient, we refine our understanding of that patient's physical and psychosocial conditions based on collection and analysis of many different types of data. *Virtual Clinical Excursions—Maternal Child Nursing* will help you develop both the creativity and the systematic approach needed to become a nurse who is equipped to deliver the highest-quality care to all patients.

REDUCING MEDICATION ERRORS

Earlier in the detailed tour, you learned the basic steps of medication preparation and administration. The following simulations will allow you to practice those skills further—with an increased emphasis on reducing medication errors by using the Medication Scorecard to evaluate your work.

Sign in to work on the Obstetrics Floor at Pacific View Regional Hospital for Period of Care 1. (*Note:* If you are already working with another patient or during another period of care, click on **Leave the Floor** and then **Restart the Program**; then sign in.)

From the Patient List, select Dorothy Grant. Then click on **Go to Nurses' Station**. Complete the following steps to prepare and administer medications to Dorothy Grant.

- Click on **Medication Room** on the tool bar at the bottom of your screen.
- Click on **MAR** and then on tab **201** to determine medications that have been ordered for Dorothy Grant. (*Note:* You may click on **Review MAR** at any time to verify the correct medication order. Always remember to check the patient name on the MAR to make sure you have the correct patient's record. You must click on the correct room number tab within the MAR.) Click on **Return to Medication Room** after reviewing the correct MAR.
- Click on **Unit Dosage** (or on the Unit Dosage cabinet); from the close-up view, click on drawer **201**.
- Select the medications you would like to administer. After each selection, click **Put Medication on Tray**. When you are finished selecting medications, click **Close Drawer** and then **View Medication Room**.
- Click **Automated System** (or on the Automated System unit itself). Click **Login**.
- On the next screen, specify the correct patient and drawer location.
- Select the medication you would like to administer and click **Put Medication on Tray**. Repeat this process if you wish to administer other medications from the Automated System.
- When you are finished, click **Close Drawer** and **View Medication Room**.
- From the Medication Room, click **Preparation** (or on the preparation tray).
- From the list of medications on your tray, highlight the correct medication to administer and click **Prepare**.
- This activates the Preparation Wizard. Supply any requested information; then click **Next**.
- Now select the correct patient to receive this medication and click **Finish**.
- Repeat the previous three steps until all medications that you want to administer are prepared.
- You can click on **Review Your Medications** and then on **Return to Medication Room** when ready. Once you are back in the Medication Room, go directly to Dorothy Grant's room by clicking on **201** at the bottom of the screen.
- Inside the patient's room, administer the medication, utilizing the six rights of medication administration. After you have collected the appropriate assessment data and are ready for administration, click **Patient Care** and then **Medication Administration**. Verify that the correct patient and medication(s) appear in the left-hand window. Highlight the first medication you wish to administer; then click the down arrow next to Select. From the drop-down menu, select **Administer** and complete the Administration Wizard by providing any information requested. When the Wizard stops asking for information, click **Administer to Patient**. Specify **Yes** when asked whether this administration should be recorded in the MAR. Finally, click **Finish**.

■ **SELF-EVALUATION**

Now let's see how you did during your medication administration!

- Click on **Leave the Floor** at the bottom of your screen. From the Floor Menu, select **Look at Your Preceptor's Evaluation**. Then click **Medication Scorecard**.

The following exercises will help you identify medication errors, investigate possible reasons for these errors, and reduce or prevent medication errors in the future.

1. Start by examining Table A. These are the medications you should have given to Dorothy Grant during this period of care. If each of the medications in Table A has a ✓ by it, then you made no errors. Congratulations!

If any medication has an X by it, then you made one or more medication errors.

Compare Tables A and B to determine which of the following types of errors you made: Wrong Dose, Wrong Route/Method/Site, or Wrong Time. Follow these steps:
   a. Find medications in Table A that were given incorrectly.
   b. Now see if those same medications are in Table B, which shows what you actually administered to Dorothy Grant.
   c. Comparing Tables A and B, match the Strength, Dose, Route/Method/Site, and Time for each medication you administered incorrectly.
   d. Then, using the form below, list the medications given incorrectly and mark the errors you made for each medication.

Medication	Strength	Dosage	Route	Method	Site	Time
	❑	❑	❑	❑	❑	❑
	❑	❑	❑	❑	❑	❑
	❑	❑	❑	❑	❑	❑
	❑	❑	❑	❑	❑	❑

2. To help you reduce future medication errors, consider the following list of possible reasons for errors.

- Did not check drug against MAR for correct medication, correct dose, correct patient, correct route, correct time, correct documentation.
- Did not check drug dose against MAR three times.
- Did not open the unit dose package in the patient's room.
- Did not correctly identify the patient using two identifiers.
- Did not administer the drug on time.
- Did not verify patient allergies.
- Did not check the patient's current condition or vital sign parameters.
- Did not consider why the patient would be receiving this drug.
- Did not question why the drug was in the patient's drawer.
- Did not check the physician's order and/or check with the pharmacist when there was a question about the drug or dose.
- Did not verify that no adverse effects had occurred from a previous dose.

Based on the list of possibilities you just reviewed, determine how you made each error and record the reason in the form below:

Medication	Reason for Error

3. Look again at Table B. Are there medications listed that are not in Table A? If so, you gave a medication to Dorothy Grant that she should not have received. Complete the following exercises to help you understand how such an error might have been made.

   a. Perhaps you gave a medication that was on Dorothy Grant's MAR for this period of care, without recognizing that a change had occurred in the patient's condition, which should have caused you to reconsider. Review patient records as necessary and complete the following form:

Medication	Possible Reasons Not to Give This Medication

   b. Another possibility is that you gave Dorothy Grant a medication that should have been given at a different time. Check her MAR and complete the form below to determine whether you made a Wrong Time error:

Medication	Given to Dorothy Grant at What Time	Should Have Been Given at What Time

c. Maybe you gave another patient's medication to Dorothy Grant. In this case, you made a Wrong Patient error. Check the MARs of other patients and use the form below to determine whether you made this type of error:

Medication	Given to Dorothy Grant	Should Have Been Given to

4. The Medication Scorecard provides some other interesting sources of information. For example, if there is a medication selected for Dorothy Grant but it was not given to her, there will be an X by that medication in Table A, but it will not appear in Table B. In that case, you might have given this medication to some other patient, which is another type of Wrong Patient error. To investigate further, look at Table D, which lists the medications you gave to other patients. See whether you can find any medications ordered for Dorothy Grant that were given to another patient by mistake. However, before you make any decisions, be sure to cross-check the MAR for other patients because the same medication may have been ordered for multiple patients. Use the following form to record your findings:

Medication	Should Have Been Given to Dorothy Grant	Given by Mistake to

5. Now take some time to review the medication exercises you just completed. Use the form below to create an overall analysis of what you have learned. Once again, record each of the medication errors you made, including the type of each error. Then, for each error you made, indicate specifically what you would do differently to prevent this type of error from occurring again.

Medication	Type of Error	Error Prevention Tactic

Submit this form to your instructor if required as a graded assignment, or simply use these exercises to improve your understanding of medication errors and how to reduce them.

Name: _____   Date: _____

Community Care: The Family and Culture

Reading Assignments:

McKinney, James, Murray, Nelson, and Ashwill: Maternal-Child Nursing, 5th edition (Chapter 3)

Perry, Hockenberry, Lowdermilk, and Wilson: Maternal Child Nursing Care, 5th edition (Chapter 2)

Patients: Dorothy Grant, Room 201
Stacey Crider, Room 202
Kelly Brady, Room 203
Maggie Gardner, Room 204
Gabriela Valenzuela, Room 205
Laura Wilson, Room 206

Objectives:

- Assess and plan care for a patient from a specific culture.
- Explore how your background influences the care that you give to patients who have differing experiences in regard to community, family, or culture.
- Discuss the various types of families, communities, and cultures represented by each of the patients.

Exercise 1

Virtual Hospital Activity

15 minutes

Review your textbook and complete the following exercise regarding family types.

Read question 1 before starting this period of care. Fill in the table as you review each patient's chart.

- Sign in to work at Pacific View Regional Hospital on the Obstetrics Floor for Period of Care 1. (*Note*: If you are already in the virtual hospital from a previous exercise, click on **Leave the Floor** and then on **Restart the Program** to get to the sign-in window.)
- From the Patient List, select all the patients to review.
- Click on **Go to Nurses' Station** and then on **Chart**.
- Click on **201** to open Dorothy Grant's chart.
- Click on **Admissions** and find the patient's marital status.
- Click on **History and Physical** and review the Family History section.
- Once you have completed the column for Dorothy Grant in the table below, click on **Return to Nurses' Station.**
- Click on **Chart** and then on **202** to open Stacey Crider's chart. Review to complete this patient's portion of the table below. Repeat this sequence until you have completed the table.

1. Under each patient's name below, place an X in the row that describes that patient's type of family. (*Note:* Some patients may require more than one X. Mark all descriptors that apply.

	Dorothy Grant	Stacey Crider	Kelly Brady	Maggie Gardner	Gabriela Valenzuela	Laura Wilson
Traditional (nuclear)						
Single-parent						
Multigenerational						
Married/Blended						
High-risk						

2. Using what you learned in your chart review, along with the information in your textbook, identify the type of family that Gabriela Valenzuela has. Briefly describe how her family fits the type you have chosen.

3. Based on the information provided in your textbook, what type of family do you have? Describe how your family fits the description of the family type that you have chosen.

Read in your textbook about various cultural and religious groups.

4. Among the Asian culture, what is one form of medicine that is widely accepted? Give an example.

5. What do Native Americans believe in regard to health?

6. How can you, as the nurse, provide the best care for any cultural group?

7. In many cultures, _____ and _____ are strongly associated.

8. Based on your review of your textbook reading, will you change your care for patients of differing cultures? If so, how? What community resources are available for patients of various cultures where you live?

Exercise 2

Virtual Hospital Activity

25 minutes

Culturally competent care is very important. As we review the various ways of providing culturally competent care, we will review two patients at Pacific View Regional Hospital.

- Sign in to work at Pacific View Regional Hospital on the Obstetrics Floor for Period of Care 1. (*Note:* If you are already in the virtual hospital from a previous exercise, click on **Leave the Floor** and then on **Restart the Program** to get to the sign-in window.)
- From the Patient List, select Stacey Crider and Maggie Gardner.
- Click on **Go to Nurses' Station**.
- Click on **Chart** and then on **202**.
- Click on **Nursing Admission** and review. (*Hint:* See the Role Relationships section.)

1. Identify nursing interventions that would be appropriate for Stacey Crider and her family in regard to culture.

Maggie Gardner and her husband are very religious. According to your textbook, most members of the African-American culture have strong feelings about family, community, and religion. With this information in mind, complete the following activity and questions.

- Click on **Return to Nurses' Station**.
- Click on **204** at the bottom of the screen.
- Click on **Patient Care** and then on **Nurse-Client Interactions**.
- Select and view the video titled **0730: Communicating Empathy**. (*Note:* Check the virtual clock to see whether enough time has elapsed. You can use the fast-forward feature to advance the time by 2-minute intervals if the video is not yet available. Then click again on **Patient Care** and **Nurse-Client Interactions** to refresh the screen.)

2. What does Maggie Gardner's husband verbalize during this interaction that would correlate with the African-American population's deep sense of religion?

3. Based on your interactions with patients in the hospital where you have worked, describe your experience(s) with caring for someone of a different culture. What are some of the ideals that are different from your own? What barriers to care have you experienced?

4. How comfortable are you with caring for patients from a different culture? Do you find yourself feeling judgmental or attempting to change others? What can you do to learn more about other cultures?

To further explore Jim and Maggie Gardner's spiritual perspective, return to the patient's chart.

- Click on **Chart** and then on **204**.
- Click on **Consultations** and review the Pastoral Care Spiritual Assessment and the Pastoral Consultation.

5. What does Maggie Gardner "blame" her miscarriages on?

6. What is Maggie Gardner's perception of God?

7. What is one underlying theme that you see in the Consultations, Nursing Admission, and History and Physical sections of the chart in regard to religion and this patient's perception of her situation?

Exercise 3

Virtual Hospital Activity

15 minutes

Just as there are different types of families, there are also various vulnerable populations or behaviors/characteristics that influence the function of the family and women within every community. To gain a better understanding of this, review relevant sections in your textbook.

Read question 1 before starting this period of care. Fill in the table as you review each patient's chart.

- Sign in to work at Pacific View Regional Hospital on the Obstetrics Floor for Period of Care 1. (*Note*: If you are already in the virtual hospital from a previous exercise, click on **Leave the Floor** and then on **Restart the Program** to get to the sign-in window.)
- From the Patient List, select all six patients.
- Click on **Go to Nurses' Station** and then on **Chart**.
- Select Dorothy Grant's chart (**201**) to begin.
- Click on **Nursing Admission**. (*Hint*: The first four pages of this section will provide information regarding the patient's population.)
- You may also click on the **History and Physical** for information to complete the table below.
- Once you have completed Dorothy Grant's column in question 1, click on **Return to Nurses' Station**. Repeat the above steps for each patient.

1. Describe each of the following individual's family dynamic/characteristic.

Dorothy Grant

Laura Wilson

Gabriela Valenzuela

Maggie Gardner

2. What has your experience been with caring for vulnerable populations?

3. Based on the information found in your textbook, will you change the way you care for these patients in the future? If so, how? In your community, what resources are available for women who are affected by the issues discussed in this exercise?

Maternal and Fetal Assessment and Nutrition

———————————————————————————

Reading Assignments:

McKinney, James, Murray, Nelson, and Ashwill: Maternal-Child Nursing, 5th edition
(Chapters 14, 15, and 26)

Perry, Hockenberry, Lowdermilk, and Wilson: Maternal Child Nursing Care, 5th edition
(Chapters 9, 10, and 11)

Patients: Kelly Brady, Room 203

Maggie Gardner, Room 204

Objectives:

- Identify appropriate interventions for maintaining adequate maternal and fetal nutrition.
- Differentiate among the varying types of assessment techniques that can be used with both low- and high-risk pregnancy patients.
- Identify various methods of testing that can be used in high-risk pregnancies.

Exercise 1

Virtual Hospital Activity

15 minutes

- Sign in to work at Pacific View Regional Hospital on the Obstetrics Floor for Period of Care 3. (*Note:* If you are already in the virtual hospital from a previous exercise, click on **Leave the Floor** and then on **Restart the Program** to get to the sign-in window.)
- From the Patient List, select Maggie Gardner.
- Click on **Go to Nurses' Station**.
- Click on **Chart** and then on **204**.
- Click on **Diagnostic Reports**.

Review information regarding ultrasounds in your textbook.

1. List at least three things that ultrasounds are used for during the first trimester.

2. List at least three things that ultrasounds are used for during the second and third trimesters.

3. What are two forms of ultrasound? When is each form used?

4. What type of ultrasound is Maggie Gardner having?

5. Based on the ultrasound findings, how large is her baby?

6. List three abnormalities found on the ultrasound in regard to the placenta.

7. What is the impression from Maggie Gardner's ultrasound in terms of the fetus and the placenta?

8. What are the recommendations regarding follow-up?

Exercise 2

Virtual Hospital Activity

15 minutes

Biophysical profile is another very important assessment tool used with patients who are experiencing a high-risk pregnancy. Review information regarding biophysical profiles in your textbook.

1. What five markers are assessed on a biophysical profile?

2. The amount of amniotic fluid provides information about _____.

3. Normal values for each of the markers listed in question 1 suggest adequate

_____ and _____.

4. Below, list the markers that are considered acute and those that are considered chronic.

Acute markers

Chronic markers

- Sign in to work at Pacific View Regional Hospital on the Obstetrics Floor for Period of Care 3. (*Note:* If you are already in the virtual hospital from a previous exercise, click on **Leave the Floor** and then on **Restart the Program** to get to the sign-in window.)
- From the Patient List, select Kelly Brady (Room 203).
- Click on **Go to Nurses' Station**.
- Click on **Chart** and then on **203**.
- Click on **Diagnostic Reports**.

5. What is the estimated gestational age of Kelly Brady's fetus?

6. What is the amniotic fluid index as indicated on the report?

7. Suppose that Kelly Brady had an abnormally low amount of amniotic fluid. What might this indicate?

8. What is the normal amniotic fluid index value?

9. What is Kelly Brady's score on the biophysical profile?

10. Based on the information you have reviewed in your textbook, what does this score indicate?

Exercise 3

Virtual Hospital Activity

15 minutes

- Sign in to work at Pacific View Regional Hospital on the Obstetrics Floor for Period of Care 1. (*Note*: If you are already in the virtual hospital from a previous exercise, click on **Leave the Floor** and then on **Restart the Program** to get to the sign-in window.)
- From the Patient List, select Maggie Gardner (Room 204).
- Click on **Go to Nurses' Station**.
- Click on **Chart** and then on **204**.
- Click on **Laboratory Reports**.

Review information regarding anemia in your textbook.

1. What were Maggie Gardner's hemoglobin and hematocrit levels on admission?

- Click on **History and Physical**.

2. What puts Maggie Gardner at a greater risk for developing anemia than the average pregnant patient? (*Hint*: Review the Genetic Screening section of her History and Physical.)

3. What complication(s) do women with anemia experience at a higher rate than those without anemia?

4. What is a normal hematocrit level for a woman who is pregnant?

5. What assessments, specifically related to an anemia diagnosis, need to be performed by the nurse at each prenatal visit?

6. According to your textbook, what are some good sources of iron that you could instruct Maggie Gardner to add to her diet?

7. Maggie Gardner is not on iron supplementation at this time; however, list at least three things that you could teach her about iron supplementation.

LESSON 3

Substance Abuse/ Intimate Partner Violence

Reading Assignments:

McKinney, James, Murray, Nelson, and Ashwill: Maternal-Child Nursing, 5th edition (Chapter 24)

Perry, Hockenberry, Lowdermilk, and Wilson: Maternal Child Nursing Care, 5th edition (Chapter 3)

Patients: Dorothy Grant, Room 201
Laura Wilson, Room 206

Objectives:

- Assess and plan care for a substance-abusing woman with a term pregnancy.
- Discuss the statistics related to intimate partner violence (IPV).
- List characteristics of battered women.
- Explore the myths and facts regarding IPV.
- Identify the nurse's role in regard to battered women or those involved in IPV.

Exercise 1

Virtual Hospital Activity

20 minutes

- Sign in to work at Pacific View Regional Hospital on the Obstetrics Floor for Period of Care 2. (*Note:* If you are already in the virtual hospital from a previous exercise, click on **Leave the Floor** and then on **Restart the Program** to get to the sign-in window.)
- From the Patient List, select Laura Wilson.
- Click on **Go to Nurses' Station**.
- Click on **Chart** and then on **206**.
- Click on **Nursing Admission**.

1. Complete the table by documenting Laura Wilson's use of alcohol and recreational drugs, based on your review of the Nursing Admission.

Substance	Reported Use
Tobacco	
Alcohol	
Marijuana	
Crack cocaine	

Read about tobacco, alcohol, marijuana, and cocaine in your textbook.

2. For each pregnancy-related risk listed in the table below, place an X under the substance(s) thought to be associated with that risk.

Pregnancy-Related Risk	Tobacco	Alcohol	Marijuana	Cocaine
Miscarriage				
Placental perfusion abnormalities				
Preterm labor/birth				
Abruptio placentae				
Fetal alcohol syndrome (FAS)				
Fetal alcohol effects (FAE)				
Stillbirth				
Fetal anomalies				
Low birth weight or fetal growth restriction				
Cognitive impairment/ learning disabilities/ developmental problems				
Perinatal mortality risk				
Sudden infant death syndrome (SIDS)				

- Click on **Return to Nurses' Station**.
- Click on **206** at the bottom of the screen.
- Click on **Patient Care** and then on **Nurse-Client Interactions**.
- Select and view the video titled **1115: Teaching—Effects of Drug Use**. (*Note:* Check the virtual clock to see whether enough time has elapsed. You can use the fast-forward feature to advance the time by 2-minute intervals if the video is not yet available. Then click on **Patient Care** and **Nurse-Client Interactions** to refresh the screen.)

3. Does Laura Wilson consider herself to be addicted? Support your answer with comments from the video.

4. How does Laura Wilson think her drug use will affect her baby?

5. According to the nurse in the video, how might Laura Wilson's drug use affect the baby?

6. Assume that you are the nurse caring for Laura Wilson today. Which interventions to deal with Laura Wilson's drug use would be most appropriate at this time?

   _____ Talk with Laura Wilson in a manner that conveys caring and concern.

   _____ Urge Laura Wilson to begin a drug treatment program today.

   _____ Explain to Laura Wilson that she may lose custody of her baby if her drug use continues.

   _____ Involve other members of the health care team in Laura Wilson's care.

7. Explain your choice(s) in question 6.

Exercise 2

Virtual Hospital Activity

30 minutes

Review the information in your textbook related to intimate partner violence.

1. According to your textbook, the estimated number of women that experience intimate partner violence

    is _____.

- Sign in to work at Pacific View Regional Hospital on the Obstetrics Floor for Period of Care 1. (*Note:* If you are already in the virtual hospital from a previous exercise, click on **Leave the Floor** and then on **Restart the Program** to get to the sign-in window.)
- From the Patient List, select Dorothy Grant.
- Click on **Go to Nurses' Station**.
- Click on **Chart** and then on **201**.
- Click on **Nursing Admission**.

In reading about Dorothy Grant's perspective on the abusive relationship she has experienced, compare and contrast this information with content regarding intimate partner violence found in your textbook.

2. What is the reality of Dorothy Grant's situation? How does that correlate with your textbook reading?

- Click on **Return to Nurses' Station**.
- Click on **201** at the bottom of the screen.
- Click on **Patient Care** and then on **Nurse-Client Interactions**.
- Select and view the video titled **0810: Monitoring/Patient Support**. (*Note:* Check the virtual clock to see whether enough time has elapsed. You can use the fast-forward feature to advance the time by 2-minute intervals if the video is not available. Then click on **Patient Care** and **Nurse-Client Interactions** to refresh the screen.)

3. In the video interaction, what does Dorothy Grant verbalize that she should do to help prevent the violence?

4. In the video, what are the patient's concerns at the moment?

- Click on **Go to Nurses' Station**.
- Click on **Chart** and then on **201**.
- Click on **Consultations** and review the Psychiatric Consult and the Social Work Consult.

Review the information regarding the myths and realities about IPV in your textbook. Based on that information and your review of Dorothy Grant's chart, answer the following questions.

5. Dorothy Grant stays in the relationship because of _____ and _____.

6. The percentage of women who are battered during pregnancy is _____.

7. Based on the information provided, in what phase of the abuse cycle is Dorothy Grant?

8. According to the consults, Dorothy Grant has several options. What are some of the options that the social worker and psychiatric heath care provider can offer her or assist her with?

9. Dorothy Grant's husband blames her for the pregnancy.
   a. True
   b. False

10. Dorothy Grant stays in the relationship because she likes to be beaten and deliberately provokes the attacks on occasion.
    a. True
    b. False

Exercise 3

Virtual Hospital Activity

20minutes

- Sign in to work at Pacific View Regional Hospital on the Obstetrics Floor for Period of Care 4. (*Note*: If you are already in the virtual hospital from a previous exercise, click on **Leave the Floor** and then **Restart the Program** to get to the sign-in window.)
- From the Nurses' Station, click on **Kardex** and then on tab **201** to review Dorothy Grant's record. (*Remember:* You are not able to visit patients or administer medications during Period of Care 4. You are able to review patient records only.)

1. What action was initiated on Wednesday to protect Dorothy Grant from her husband?

2. What care plan interventions would be appropriate for this patient's current life situation?

3. What other disciplines have been contacted or consulted that will ensure continuity of care for Dorothy Grant as it relates to her abuse?

4. As a nurse caring for Dorothy Grant, what is your responsibility for reporting IPV?

5. What are the reporting requirements of the state in which you practice?

6. What are the resources available in your area for women who have experienced intimate partner violence?

4 _____

Reproductive Concerns, Infertility, and Contraception

_____

Reading Assignments:

McKinney, James, Murray, Nelson, and Ashwill: Maternal-Child Nursing, 5th edition
(Chapters 11 and 31)
Perry, Hockenberry, Lowdermilk, and Wilson: Maternal Child Nursing Care, 5th edition
(Chapters 3, 4, and 5)

Patients: Stacey Crider, Room 202
Kelly Brady, Room 203
Maggie Gardner, Room 204
Gabriela Valenzuela, Room 205
Laura Wilson, Room 206

Objectives:

- Identify reproductive concerns that can occur.
- Differentiate among the varying types of contraception available.
- Identify various methods of testing and treatment options that can be used for couples experiencing infertility concerns.

Exercise 1

Virtual Hospital Activity

10 minutes

Review information in your textbook.

1. What is a normal length for a menstrual cycle?

Approximately 28 days, but it can range from 20-45 days.

2. What are the criteria required to diagnose an individual with amenorrhea? Differentiate between primary and secondary amenorrhea.

Primary — when the girl doesn't reach menarche by the age which is normal. Secondary — the cessation of menstruation for 6 months or more after having regular periods.

- Sign in to work at Pacific View Regional Hospital on the Obstetrics Floor for Period of Care 1. (*Note:* If you are already in the virtual hospital from a previous exercise, click on **Leave the Floor** and then on **Restart the Program** to get to the sign-in window.)
- From the Patient List, select Stacey Crider (Room 202).
- Click on **Go to Nurses' Station**.
- Click on **Chart** and then on **202**.
- Click on **History and Physical**.
- Review the patient's gynecologic history. (*Hint:* See the bottom of page 1.)

3. Does Stacey Crider meet the textbook criteria for amenorrhea?

No

4. What is her history?

Menarche @ age 10 with irregular, sometimes months apart, periods.

5. List three things that can cause amenorrhea.

Strenuous exercise
Inadequate nutrition
Eating Disorders

Exercise 2

Virtual Hospital Activity

20 minutes

Review your textbook.

1. What is contraception?

The prevention of pregnancy

2. What is the primary focus of counseling when recommending/evaluating methods of contraception?

Provide current and correct information

- Sign in to work at Pacific View Regional Hospital on the Obstetrics Floor for Period of Care 1. (*Note*: If you are already in the virtual hospital from a previous exercise, click on **Leave the Floor** and then on **Restart the Program** to get to the sign-in window.)
- From the Patient List, select Kelly Brady, Gabriela Valenzuela, and Laura Wilson.
- Click on **Go to Nurses' Station**.
- Click on **Chart** and then on **203** for Kelly Brady's chart.
- Review the **History and Physical**.
- Repeat the previous three steps for Gabriela Valenzuela (Room 205) and Laura Wilson (Room 206).

3. Identify the birth control method each woman was using prior to her current pregnancy.

Kelly Brady

Oral contraceptives for 10 years

Gabriela Valenzuela

None

Laura Wilson

BCP's for one year @ age 16

4. Gabriela Valenzuela is Catholic. Which method would be appropriate for the nurse to discuss with her?

Condoms or BCP's if they are open to it. Otherwise natural family planning.

5. What does this method rely on?

Having sex during the infertile period of a woman's cycle.

6. Kelly Brady wants to use oral contraceptives while breastfeeding to prevent pregnancy. Which type of oral contraception is appropriate for her to use? Why?

Progestin Only Pills. They won't decrease milk production.

7. Laura Wilson is HIV-positive. What is the most appropriate form of birth control for her? Why?

Condoms. It protects the partner from transmitting HIV.

Exercise 3

Virtual Hospital Activity

20 minutes

Review your textbook.

1. Up to __15__ % of women of reproductive age have a problem with infertility.

2. When a woman reaches her ___Menopause___, a natural decline in fertility begins.

3. List four factors that affect male fertility.

Sperm abnormalities
abnormal erections
abnormal ejaculation
Seminal Fluid abnormalities

4. List at least three factors that affect female fertility.

Ovulation disorders
Fallopian tube abnormalities
Cervix abnormalities

- Sign in to work at Pacific View Regional Hospital on the Obstetrics Floor for Period of Care 1. (*Note*: If you are already in the virtual hospital from a previous exercise, click on **Leave the Floor** and then on **Restart the Program** to get to the sign-in window.)
- From the Patient List, select Maggie Gardner (Room 204).
- Click on **Go to Nurses' Station**.
- Click on **Chart** and then on **204**.
- Review the **History and Physical**.

5. Maggie Gardner was married __3½__ years before she conceived the first time.

6. Based on your textbook reading, which of the following would Maggie Gardner have been diagnosed with if she had chosen to get treatment after 1 year of attempting to get pregnant?
   a. Primary infertility
   b. Secondary infertility

7. List at least three tests that can be completed on a male patient to determine the causes of infertility?

Hormone evaluations
Semen analysis
Testicular biopsy

8. List at least four tests that can be completed on a female patient to determine the causes of infertility?

Basal Body Temp.
Cervical mucus evaluation
Hormone evaluations
Ultrasound imaging

9. What test is used to assess a couple to determine adequacy of cervical mucus and sperm function after sexual intercourse has occurred?

Post coital Test

10. What methods are available to assist an infertile couple to conceive?

Medications, Surgery, Therapeutic insemination, egg donation, surrogate parently, IUF, GIFT, ZIFT, ICSI

11. Which methods did Maggie Gardner and her husband use to assist in getting pregnant? (*Hint*: Review the OB history in the History and Physical.)

None

12. What has your experience been with a couple and their infertility experience as it relates to cultural or religious practices? Reflect on what you have learned about the culture or religious group practices as it relates to childbearing.

I honestly have no such experience.

Sexually Transmitted and Other Infections

Reading Assignments:

McKinney, James, Murray, Nelson, and Ashwill: Maternal-Child Nursing, 5th edition (Chapter 26)

Perry, Hockenberry, Lowdermilk, and Wilson: Maternal Child Nursing Care, 5th edition (Chapter 4)

Patients: Stacey Crider, Room 202

Gabriela Valenzuela, Room 205

Laura Wilson, Room 206

Objectives:

- Assess and plan care for a pregnant woman with bacterial vaginosis.
- Explain the importance of prophylactic Group B streptococcus treatment.
- Identify risk factors for acquiring HIV infection.
- Prioritize information to be included in patient teaching related to HIV infection.

Exercise 1

Virtual Hospital Activity

15 minutes

- Sign in to work at Pacific View Regional Hospital on the Obstetrics Floor for Period of Care 1. (*Note*: If you are already in the virtual hospital from a previous exercise, click on **Leave the Floor** and then on **Restart the Program** to get to the sign-in window.)
- From the Patient List, select Stacey Crider (Room 202).
- Click on **Go to Nurses' Station**.
- Click on **Chart** and then on **202**.
- Click on **History and Physical**.

1. In the table below, describe Stacey Crider's vaginal discharge based on her diagnosis on admission. How does it compare with the description of bacterial vaginosis found in your textbook?

	Stacey Crider's Discharge	Textbook Description
Appearance		
Amount		
Odor		

2. How is bacterial vaginosis diagnosed?

3. Which medication is recommended for treating bacterial vaginosis during pregnancy?

- Now click on **Physician's Orders** in the chart.
- Scroll down to the admitting physician's orders on Tuesday at 0630.

4. What are Stacey Crider's admission diagnoses?

5. Explain how Stacey Crider's admission diagnoses are likely to be related.

6. Which medication did Stacey Crider's physician order to treat her bacterial vaginosis?

7. Assume that Stacey Crider is discharged home on day 4 of the prescribed treatment with the medication you identified in question 6. What specific information about this medication should she be taught?

- Click on **Return to Nurses' Station**.

Exercise 2

Virtual Hospital Activity

15 minutes

- Sign in to work at Pacific View Regional Hospital on the Obstetrics Floor for Period of Care 1. (*Note:* If you are already in the virtual hospital from a previous exercise, click on **Leave the Floor** and then on **Restart the Program** to get to the sign-in window.)
- From the Patient List, select Gabriela Valenzuela (Room 205).
- Click on **Go to Nurses' Station**.
- Click on **Chart** and then on **205**.
- Click on **History and Physical** and scroll to the plan at the end of this document.

1. What is the medical plan of care for Gabriela Valenzuela?

2. Is Gabriela Valenzuela known to be positive for Group B streptococcus (GBS)?

Read about Group B streptococcus in your textbook; then answer questions 3 through 6.

3. List risk factors for neonatal GBS infection. Which risk factor applies to Gabriela Valenzuela?

4. Because pregnant women with GBS in the vagina are almost always asymptomatic, why does Gabriela Valenzuela need to be treated for this organism?

- Click on **Physician's Orders**.
- Scroll to the admission orders written Tuesday at 2100.

5. What medication/dosage/frequency will Gabriela Valenzuela receive for Group B strep prophylaxis?

6. How does this order compare with the treatment regimen recommended in your textbook?

- Click on **Return to Nurses' Station**.

Exercise 3

Virtual Hospital Activity

35 minutes

- Sign in to work at Pacific View Regional Hospital on the Obstetrics Floor for Period of Care 1. (*Note:* If you are already in the virtual hospital from a previous exercise, click on **Leave the Floor** and then on **Restart the Program** to get to the sign-in window.)
- From the Patient List, select Laura Wilson (Room 206).
- Click on **Go to Nurses' Station**.
- Click on **Chart** and then on **206**.
- Click on **Nursing Admission**.

1. What risk factors for acquiring an STI are identified on Laura Wilson's Nursing Admission form?

2. List specific risk factors for acquiring HIV infection. (*Hint:* See your textbook.) Place an asterisk next to the risk factors that are present in Laura Wilson's history.

3. What did the admitting nurse document about Laura Wilson's knowledge and acceptance of her HIV diagnosis?

- Click on **Return to Nurses' Station** and then on **206** at the bottom of the screen.
- Click on **Patient Care** and then **Nurse-Client Interactions**.
- Select and view the video titled **0800: Teaching—HIV in Pregnancy**. (*Note:* Check the virtual clock to see whether enough time has elapsed. You can use the fast-forward feature to advance the time by 2-minute intervals if the video is not yet available. Then click on **Patient Care** and **Nurse-Client Interactions** to refresh the screen.)

4. Does Laura Wilson appear to be fully aware of the implications of HIV infection? State the rationale for your answer.

5. What coping mechanism is Laura Wilson exhibiting in the video interaction?

- Click on **Chart** and then on **206**.
- Click on **Nursing Admission**.

6. Laura Wilson needs education on all of the following topics. Which would you choose to teach her about at this time?

_____ Safer sex

_____ Medication side effects and importance of compliance

_____ Need for medical follow-up and medication for the baby

_____ Impact of HIV on birth plans

7. Give a rationale for your answer to question 6.

Disorders During Pregnancy: Cardiac, Lupus

Reading Assignments:

McKinney, James, Murray, Nelson, and Ashwill: Maternal-Child Nursing, 5th edition (Chapter 26)

Perry, Hockenberry, Lowdermilk, and Wilson: Maternal Child Nursing Care, 5th edition (Chapter 11)

Patients: Maggie Gardner, Room 204

Gabriela Valenzuela, Room 205

Objectives:

• Identify appropriate interventions for managing selected medical-surgical problems in pregnancy.

• Plan and evaluate essential patient education during the acute phase of diagnosis.

Exercise 1

Virtual Hospital Activity

10 minutes

• Sign in to work at Pacific View Regional Hospital on the Obstetrics Floor for Period of Care 1. (*Note:* If you are already in the virtual hospital from a previous exercise, click on **Leave the Floor** and then on **Restart the Program** to get to the sign-in window.)

• From the Patient List, select Gabriela Valenzuela (Room 205).

• Click on **Go to Nurses' Station**.

• Click on **Chart** and then on **205**.

• Click on **History and Physical**.

Review material regarding cardiac problems during pregnancy in your textbook.

1. In the History and Physical for Gabriela Valenzuela, what does the physician note as her cardiac problem?

2. Mitral valve disease is one of the most common causes of cardiac disease in pregnant women.
   a. True
   b. False

3. According to the History and Physical, what cardiac symptoms does Gabriela Valenzuela exhibit now that she is pregnant?

4. Based on your textbook reading, why do women with cardiac disorders have problems during their pregnancy?

5. What abnormal assessment finding is noted in the History and Physical that would be associated with Gabriela Valenzuela's cardiac disorder?

Exercise 2

Virtual Hospital Activity

20 minutes

Autoimmune disorders encompass a wide variety of disorders that can be disruptive to the pregnancy process. Maggie Gardner has been admitted to rule out systemic lupus erythematosus (SLE). The following activities will explore the various aspects of this autoimmune disorder. Review the information regarding SLE in your textbook.

- Sign in to work at Pacific View Regional Hospital on the Obstetrics Floor for Period of Care 1. (*Note:* If you are already in the virtual hospital from a previous exercise, click on **Leave the Floor** and then on **Restart the Program** to get to the sign-in window.)
- From the Patient List, select Maggie Gardner (Room 204).
- Click on **Go to Nurses' Station**.
- Click on **Chart** and then on **204**.
- Click on **History and Physical**.

1. Based on Maggie Gardner's History and Physical, what information would correlate to a diagnosis of SLE?

2. According to your textbook, what are the most common presenting symptoms of this disease during pregnancy?

- Click on **Return to Nurses' Station**.
- Click on **204** at the bottom of the screen.
- Click on **Patient Care** and then on **Physical Assessment**.
- Click on the various body system categories (yellow buttons) and subcategories (green buttons) to perform a head-to-toe assessment of Maggie Gardner.

3. Based on your head-to-toe assessment, list four abnormal findings that are related to Maggie Gardner's diagnosis.

- Click on **Chart** and then on **204**.
- Click on **Patient Education**.

4. Based on your physical assessment, the information from the Patient Education section of the chart, and the fact that this is a new diagnosis for the patient, list three areas of teaching that need to be completed with this patient.

Exercise 3

Virtual Hospital Activity

35 minutes

- Sign in to work at Pacific View Regional Hospital on the Obstetrics Floor for Period of Care 3. (*Note*: If you are already in the virtual hospital from a previous exercise, click on **Leave the Floor** and then on **Restart the Program** to get to the sign-in window.)
- From the Patient List, select Maggie Gardner (Room 204).
- Click on **Go to Nurses' Station**.
- Click on **Chart** and then on **204**.
- Click on **Consultations** and review the Rheumatology Consult.

1. List four things noted in the rheumatologist impressions regarding specific findings that are associated with a diagnosis of SLE for Maggie Gardner.

- Click on **Diagnostic Reports**.

2. Maggie Gardner had an ultrasound done before the consultation with the rheumatologist. What were the findings as they relate to SLE? What were the follow-up recommendations? (*Hint*: See Impressions section.)

3. What is the rheumatologist's plan regarding laboratory/diagnostics to gain a definitive diagnosis?

4. According to the Rheumatology Consult, what is the plan regarding medications (immediate need)?

- Click on **Return to Nurses' Station**.
- Click on the **Drug** icon in the lower left corner of the screen.
- Find the Drug Guide profile of prednisone. (*Hint:* You can type the drug name in the Search box or scroll through the alphabetic list of drugs at the top of the screen.)

5. What does Maggie Gardner need to be taught regarding this medication?

- Click on **Return to Nurses' Station**.
- Click on **204**.
- Click on **Patient Care** and then on **Nurse-Client Interactions**.
- Select and view the video titled **1530: Disease Management**. (*Note:* Check the virtual clock to see whether enough time has elapsed. You can use the fast-forward feature to advance the time by 2-minute intervals if the video is not yet available. Then click on **Patient Care** and **Nurse-Client Interactions** to refresh the screen.)

6. During this video, the nurse provides Maggie Gardner with information regarding her disease. What two things does the nurse note that are important aspects of the patient's disease management during pregnancy?

7. What medication, ordered by the rheumatologist, will assist in the blood flow to the placenta? How?

8. What key component does the nurse identify for Maggie Gardner that will assist in maintaining a healthy pregnancy?

9. What excuse does Maggie Gardner provide for not keeping previous doctors' appointments? (*Hint:* This information is also found in the Nursing Admission in the chart.)

Exercise 4

Virtual Hospital Activity

15 minutes

- Sign in to work at Pacific View Regional Hospital on the Obstetrics Floor for Period of Care 4. (*Note*: If you are already in the virtual hospital from a previous exercise, click on **Leave the Floor** and then on **Restart the Program** to get to the sign-in window.)
- From the Nurses' Station, click on **Chart**. (*Remember:* You are not able to visit patients or administer medications during Period of Care 4. You are able to review patient records only.)
- Click on **204** to open Maggie Gardner's chart.
- Click on **Laboratory Reports**.

1. The results are now available for the following laboratory tests that were ordered for Maggie Gardner during Period of Care 2. What are the findings?

Laboratory Test	Maggie Gardner's Result
C3	
C4	
CH50	
RPR	
ANA titer	
Anticardiolipin	
Anti-sm; Anti-DNA; Anti-SSA	
Anti-SSB	
Anti-RVV; Antiphospholipid	

- Click on **Consultations** and review the Rheumatology Consult.

2. The lab findings you recorded in question 1 are definitive for the diagnosis of SLE. According to your textbook and the Rheumatology Consult, what is the plan to manage this disease once Maggie Gardner's baby is delivered?

- Click on **Nurse's Notes.**

3. By Period of Care 4, Maggie Gardner has been provided with education regarding various aspects of her disease process, testing, and hospital procedures. Based on your review of the Nurse's Notes for Wednesday, what has she been specifically taught? Include the time each topic of instruction took place.

4. List three possible patient problems for Maggie Gardner.

5. SLE requires long-term management because patients will experience remissions and exacerbations. What step did the rheumatologist take with Maggie Gardner to begin the long-term relationship that will be required to ensure a healthy outcome?

Disorders During Pregnancy: Diabetes Mellitus

Reading Assignments:

McKinney, James, Murray, Nelson, and Ashwill: Maternal-Child Nursing, 5th edition (Chapter 26)

Perry, Hockenberry, Lowdermilk, and Wilson: Maternal Child Nursing Care, 5th edition (Chapter 11)

Patient: Stacey Crider, Room 202

Objectives:

- Identify appropriate interventions for controlling hyperglycemia in a patient with gestational diabetes mellitus (GDM).
- Correctly administer insulin to a patient with GDM.
- Plan and evaluate essential patient teaching for a patient with GDM.

Exercise 1

Virtual Hospital Activity

30 minutes

- Sign in to work at Pacific View Regional Hospital on the Obstetrics Floor for Period of Care 2. (*Note*: If you are already in the virtual hospital from a previous exercise, click on **Leave the Floor** and then on **Restart the Program** to get to the sign-in window.)
- From the Patient List, select Stacey Crider (Room 202).
- Click on **Go to Nurses' Station**.
- Click on **Chart** and then on **202**.
- Click on **History and Physical**.

1. When was Stacey Crider's GDM diagnosed? How has it been managed thus far?

2. Read about risk factors for GDM in your textbook. List these factors below.

- To search for evidence of the above risk factors in Stacey Crider, continue reviewing her History and Physical and then click on and review her **Nursing Admissions**.

3. Which risk factors for GDM are present in Stacey Crider?

4. What does Stacey Crider's physician suspect is the cause of her poorly controlled blood glucose levels? (*Hint*: See the Impression section at the end of her History and Physical.)

- Click on **Physician's Orders**.

5. Look at Stacey Crider's admission orders. Write down the orders that are related to GDM.

6. Why did Stacey Crider's physician order an HbA$_{1C}$ test as part of her admission labs? (*Hint*: See your textbook.)

On admission, Stacey Crider is in preterm labor. This was treated with magnesium sulfate tocolysis. She was also given a course of betamethasone.

- Click on **Return to Nurses' Station**.
- Click on the **Drug** icon in the lower left corner of the screen.
- Use the search box or scroll bar to find the entry for betamethasone.

7. How might betamethasone affect Stacey Crider's GDM?

- Click on **Return to Nurses' Station**.
- Click on **Chart** and then on **202**.
- Click on **Physician's Notes**.
- Scroll to the note for Tuesday at 0700.

8. How does Stacey Crider's physician plan to deal with these potential medication effects?

Stacey Crider's other admission diagnosis is bacterial vaginosis (BV).

- Click on **Return to Nurses' Station**.
- Click on **202** at the bottom of the screen.
- Click on **Patient Care** and then on **Nurse-Client Interactions**.
- Select and view the video titled **1115: Teaching—Diet, Infection**. (*Note:* Check the virtual clock to see whether enough time has elapsed. You can use the fast-forward feature to advance the time by 2-minute intervals if the video is not yet available. Then click on **Patient Care** and **Nurse-Client Interactions** to refresh the screen.)

9. What is the relationship between Stacey Crider's bacterial vaginosis infection and her GDM?

Exercise 2

Virtual Hospital Activity

20 minutes

- Sign in to work at Pacific View Regional Hospital on the Obstetrics Floor for Period of Care 1. (*Note*: If you are already in the virtual hospital from a previous exercise, click on **Leave the Floor** and then on **Restart the Program** to get to the sign-in window.)
- From the Patient List, select Stacey Crider (Room 202).
- Click on **Go to Nurses' Station**.
- Click on the **Drug** icon in the lower left corner.

Stacey Crider needs her insulin so that she can eat breakfast. Remember that she receives lispro insulin prior to each meal and NPH insulin at bedtime. Read about the different types of insulin in the Drug Guide.

1. Using the information found in the Pharmacokinetics section of the entry for insulin in the Drug Guide, complete the table below.

Type of Insulin	Onset of Action	Peak	Duration
Lispro			
Intermediate-acting			

Read about proper insulin injection technique in your textbook.

- Click on **EPR** and then on **Login**.
- Select **202** from the Patient drop-down menu and **Vital Signs** from the Category drop-down menu.
- Look at the vital sign assessment documented on Wednesday at 0700.

2. What was Stacey Crider's blood glucose?

- Click on **Exit EPR**.
- Click on **MAR**.
- Click on tab **202**.

3. What is Stacey Crider's prescribed insulin dosage?

- Click on **Return to Nurses' Station**.
- Click on **Chart** and then on **202**.
- Click on **Physician's Orders** and scroll to the orders for Tuesday at 1900.

4. How much insulin should Stacey Crider receive? Why?

- Click on **Return to Nurses' Station**.
- Click on **Medication Room**.
- Click on **Unit Dosage**.
- Click on drawer **202**.
- Click on **Insulin Lispro**.
- Click on **Put Medication on Tray**.
- Click on **Close Drawer**.
- Click on **View Medication Room**.
- Click on **Preparation**.
- Click on **Prepare** and follow the prompts to complete preparation of Stacey Crider's lispro insulin dose.
- Click on **Return to Medication Room**.

You are almost ready to give Stacey Crider's insulin injection. However, before you do . . .

5. Considering lispro insulin's rapid onset of action, what else should you check before giving Stacey Crider her injection?

Now you're ready!

- Click on **202**.
- Click on **Check Armband**.
- Click on **Patient Care**.
- Click on **Medication Administration**.
- Insulin Lispro should be listed on the left side of your screen. Click on the down arrow next to **Select** and choose **Administer**.
- Follow the prompts to administer Stacey Crider's insulin injection. Indicate **Yes** to document the injection in the MAR.
- Click on **Leave the Floor**.
- Click on **Look at Your Preceptor's Evaluation**.
- Click on **Medication Scorecard**.

How did you do?

Exercise 3

Virtual Hospital Activity

30 minutes

- Sign in to work at Pacific View Regional Hospital on the Obstetrics Floor for Period of Care 3. (*Note*: If you are already in the virtual hospital from a previous exercise, click on **Leave the Floor** and then on **Restart the Program** to get to the sign-in window.)
- From the Patient List, select Stacey Crider (Room 202).
- Click on **Go to Nurses' Station**.
- Click on **Chart** and then on **202**.
- Click on **Patient Education**.

Stacey Crider will likely be discharged home soon. Review her Patient Education record to determine her learning needs in relation to GDM.

1. List the educational goals for Stacey Crider regarding GDM.

Read about nursing care of pregnant women with DM in your textbook.

2. Which of Stacey Crider's educational goals would *not* apply to all women with GDM? Support your answer.

- Click on **Nurse's Notes** and scroll to the note for 0600 Wednesday.

3. How did the nurse describe Stacey Crider's ability to give her own insulin injection at that time?

- Click again on **Patient Education**.

4. What teaching has already been done with this patient on Wednesday in regard to GDM?

- Click on **Nurse's Notes** and scroll to the note for 1200 Wednesday.

5. Do you think today's initial teaching on insulin administration was effective? Support your answer using objective documentation from the Nurse's Note.

Use the information you have obtained from the Patient Education form and the Nurse's Notes to answer the following questions.

6. Teaching goals for Stacey Crider include all of the following. Which goal(s) would you choose to work on with her during *this* period of care? Select all that apply.

_____ Verbalize appropriate food choices and portions.

_____ Demonstrate good technique when administering insulin.

_____ Demonstrate good technique with self-monitoring of blood glucose.

_____ Recognize hyper- and hypoglycemia and how to treat each.

7. Give a rationale for your answer to question 6.

8. Which goal do you think Stacey Crider would choose to work on during this period of care?

_____ Verbalize appropriate food choices and portions.

_____ Demonstrate good technique when administering insulin.

_____ Demonstrate good technique with self-monitoring of blood glucose.

_____ Recognize hyper- and hypoglycemia and how to treat each.

9. Give a rationale for your answer to question 8.

Read about risk factors for GDM in your textbook.

10. Stacey Crider has a significant risk for developing glucose intolerance later in life. What advice would you give her to reduce this risk?

11. Because she has had GDM with this pregnancy, what medical follow-up would you advise for Stacey Crider after her baby is born? Why?

12. Do you believe Stacey Crider's GDM might affect her child? What advice would you give her regarding medical follow-up for her baby?

LESSON 8

Disorders During Pregnancy: Hypertension

Reading Assignments:

McKinney, James, Murray, Nelson, and Ashwill: Maternal-Child Nursing, 5th edition (Chapter 25)

Perry, Hockenberry, Lowdermilk, and Wilson: Maternal Child Nursing Care, 5th edition (Chapter 12)

Patient: Kelly Brady, Room 203

Objectives:

- Assess and identify signs and symptoms present in the patient with severe preeclampsia.
- Explain how common signs and symptoms present in the patient with severe preeclampsia relate to the underlying pathophysiology of this disease.
- Identify the patient who has developed HELLP syndrome.
- Describe routine nursing care for the patient with severe preeclampsia who is receiving magnesium sulfate.

Exercise 1

Virtual Hospital Activity

20 minutes

- Sign in to work at Pacific View Regional Hospital on the Obstetrics Floor for Period of Care 3. (*Note*: If you are already in the virtual hospital from a previous exercise, click on **Leave the Floor** and then on **Restart the Program** to get to the sign-in window.)
- From the Patient List, select Kelly Brady (Room 203).
- Click on **Go to Nurses' Station**.
- Click on **Chart** and then on **203**.
- Click on **History and Physical**.

1. What was Kelly Brady's admission diagnosis?

2. Using Kelly Brady's History and Physical, as well as your textbook, complete the table below.

Sign/Symptom	Mild Preeclampsia	Severe Preeclampsia	Kelly Brady on Admission
Blood pressure			
Proteinuria			
Headache			
Visual problems			
Right upper quadrant or epigastric pain			

- Click on **Physician's Orders** and find the admitting physician's orders on Tuesday at 1030.

3. What tests and/or procedures did Kelly Brady's physician order to confirm the diagnosis of severe preeclampsia?

- Click on **Physician's Notes** and scroll to the note for Wednesday 0730.

4. What subjective and objective data are recorded here that would support the diagnosis of severe preeclampsia?

Kelly Brady's 24-hour urine collection was completed and sent to the lab at 1230.

- Click on **Laboratory Reports**.
- Scroll to find the Wednesday 1230 results.

5. Below, record the results of Kelly Brady's 24-hour urine collection.

6. Now list all the data you have collected during this exercise that confirm Kelly Brady's diagnosis of severe preeclampsia.

Exercise 2

Virtual Hospital Activity

20 minutes

- Sign in to work at Pacific View Regional Hospital on the Obstetrics Floor for Period of Care 1. (*Note*: If you are already in the virtual hospital from a previous exercise, click on **Leave the Floor** and then on **Restart the Program** to get to the sign-in window.)
- From the Patient List, select Kelly Brady (Room 203).
- Click on **Go to Nurses' Station**.
- Click on **203** at the bottom of the screen to go to the patient's room.
- Click on **Take Vital Signs**.

1. Record Kelly Brady's vital signs for 0730.

- Now click on **Patient Care**. To perform a focused assessment, select the various body system categories (yellow buttons) and subcategories (green buttons) as listed in question 2.

2. Record your findings from the focused assessment of Kelly Brady in the table below.

Assessment Area	Kelly Brady's Findings
Head and Neck 　Sensory	
Neurologic	
Chest 　Respiratory	
Abdomen 　Gastrointestinal	
Lower Extremities 　Neurologic	

3. Match each of the signs or symptoms below with the preeclampsia-associated pathology it indicates. (*Note:* Some letters will be used more than once.)

_____ Blurred vision/blind spots

_____ Headache

_____ Epigastric pain

_____ Hyperreflexia

_____ Elevated blood pressure

_____ Proteinuria/oliguria

a. Generalized vasoconstriction

b. Glomerular damage

c. Vasoconstriction of cerebral vessels; arteriolar spasms

d. Hepatic edema and subcapsular hemorrhage; hemorrhagic necrosis

Exercise 3

Virtual Hospital Activity

30 minutes

• Sign in to work at Pacific View Regional Hospital on the Obstetrics Floor for Period of Care 3. (*Note*: If you are already in the virtual hospital from a previous exercise, click on **Leave the Floor** and then on **Restart the Program** to get to the sign-in window.)
• From the Patient List, select Kelly Brady (Room 203).
• Click on **Go to Nurses' Station**.

Read about HELLP syndrome in your textbook.

1. Why do you think Kelly Brady had blood drawn at 1230 for an AST measurement and a platelet count?

• Click on **Chart** and then on **203**.
• Click on **Laboratory Reports**.
• Scroll to the report for Wednesday 1230 to locate the results of these tests.

2. Complete the table below based on your review of the Laboratory Reports and your textbook.

Test	Wednesday 1230 Result	Value in HELLP
Platelet count		
AST		

• Click on **Return to Nurses' Station**.
• Click on **Patient List** on the tool bar at the top of the screen.
• Click on **Get Report** for Kelly Brady.

3. Why has Kelly Brady been transferred to labor and delivery?

4. What does the acronym HELLP mean?

- Click on **Return to Patient List** and then on **Return to Nurses' Station**.
- Click on **Chart** and then on **203**.
- Click on **Physician's Notes**.
- Scroll to the note for Wednesday 1530.

5. What is the physician's plan of care for Kelly Brady, in light of the HELLP syndrome diagnosis?

Assume that you will be the nurse caring for Kelly Brady after her surgery while she is receiving magnesium sulfate. Read about this medication in your textbook and then answer question 6.

6. All of the assessments/interventions listed below are part of routine nursing care for a patient with severe preeclampsia. Which of these are performed specifically to assess for magnesium toxicity? Select all that apply.

_____ Measure/record urine output.

_____ Measure proteinuria using urine dipstick.

_____ Monitor liver enzyme levels and platelet count.

_____ Monitor for headache, visual disturbances, and epigastric pain.

_____ Assess for decreased level of consciousness.

_____ Assess DTRs.

_____ Weigh daily to assess for edema.

_____ Monitor vital signs, especially respiratory rate.

_____ Dim room lights and maintain a quiet environment.

Disorders During Pregnancy: Hemorrhagic Disorders

Reading Assignments:

McKinney, James, Murray, Nelson, and Ashwill: Maternal-Child Nursing, 5th edition (Chapter 25)

Perry, Hockenberry, Lowdermilk, and Wilson: Maternal Child Nursing Care, 5th edition (Chapter 12)

Patient: Gabriela Valenzuela, Room 205

Objectives:

- Identify appropriate interventions for managing abruptio placentae.
- Differentiate between the symptoms related to an abruptio placentae and those related to a placenta previa.
- Plan and evaluate essential patient education during the acute phase of diagnosis.

Exercise 1

Virtual Hospital Activity

45 minutes

- Sign in to work at Pacific View Regional Hospital on the Obstetrics Floor for Period of Care 1. (*Note*: If you are already in the virtual hospital from a previous exercise, click on **Leave the Floor** and then on **Restart the Program** to get to the sign-in window.)
- From the Patient List, select Gabriela Valenzuela (Room 205).
- Click on **Go to Nurses' Station**.
- Click on **Chart** and then on **205**.
- Click on **Emergency Department**.

1. What happened that precipitated Gabriela Valenzuela coming to the Emergency Department? How long did she wait before actually coming? What was the deciding factor in her coming to the Emergency Department?

Read about the incidence and etiology of abruptio placentae in your textbook.

2. Other than a motor vehicle accident, what could result in or increase the risk for having an abruptio placentae?

3. Differential diagnosis is very important when you are confronted with clinical manifestations that could be evidence of more than one process. Based on the information in your textbook, compare and contrast abruptio placentae and placenta previa in the table below.

Characteristic/Complication	Abruptio Placentae	Placenta Previa
Bleeding		
Shock complication		
Coagulopathy (DIC)		
Uterine tonicity		
Tenderness/pain		
Placenta findings		
Fetal effects		

4. Based on your review of the Emergency Department report in the chart, what type of abruption does Gabriela Valenzuela have? Provide supporting documentation from your textbook reading.

- Click on **Return to Nurses' Station**.
- Click on **205** to go to the patient's room.
- Click on **Patient Care** and then on **Nurse-Client Interactions**.
- Select and view the video titled **0740: Patient Teaching—Fetal Monitoring**. (*Note:* Check the virtual clock to see whether enough time has elapsed. You can use the fast-forward feature to advance the time by 2-minute intervals if the video is not yet available. Then click on **Patient Care** and **Nurse-Client Interactions** to refresh the screen.)

5. Once Gabriela Valenzuela is admitted to the floor, what are her and her husband's concerns? What does the nurse include in her teaching to alleviate those concerns?

Gabriela Valenzuela is at increased risk for early delivery as a result of the abdominal trauma she suffered and the subsequent occurrence of a grade 1 abruptio placentae. She is currently manifesting signs and symptoms of early labor. According to the Physician's Orders, she was given a dose of betamethasone, which is to be repeated in 12 hours.

6. What is the purpose of the administration of betamethasone in this patient's case? (*Hint*: Review information in your textbook.)

- Click on **MAR** and review the betamethasone dosage to be given to Gabriela Valenzuela.
- Click on **Return to Room 205**.
- Click on **Medication Room**.
- Click on **Unit Dosage**.
- Click on drawer **205**.
- Click on **Betamethasone** in the upper left corner of the screen.
- Click on **Put Medication on Tray**.
- Click on **Close Drawer**.
- Click on **View Medication Room**.
- Click on **Preparation**.
- Click on **Prepare** and follow the Preparation Wizard's prompts to complete preparation of Gabriela Valenzuela's betamethasone.
- When the Wizard stops asking questions, click on **Finish**.
- Click on **Return to Medication Room**.
- Click on **205** to return to the patient's room.
- Click on **Patient Care**.
- Click on **Medication Administration**.
- Click on **Review Your Medications**.
- Click on the tab marked **Prepared**.

7. According to the text box on the right side of your screen, what is the medication name and dosage that you have prepared for Gabriela Valenzuela?

8. Based on your answer to the previous question, how many milligrams are you giving to Gabriela Valenzuela? Is this the correct dosage based on the MAR?

- Click on **Return to Room 205**.
- Click on the **Drug** icon in the left-hand corner of the screen.
- To read about betamethasone, either type the drug name in the search box or scroll through the alphabetic list of medications at the top of the screen.

9. Based on the information provided in the Drug Guide, what is the indication and dosage for pregnant adults?

10. Based on your review of the baseline assessment data in the Drug Guide, what areas need to be assessed in Gabriela Valenzuela's history?

11. Now review the information regarding the administration of this medication. What are three things that need to be taken into consideration when giving this medication in the injection form?

12. What are the six rights of medication administration as they relate to the patient?

You are now ready to complete the medication administration.

- Click on **Return to Room 205**.
- Click on **Check Armband**.
- Within the purple box under the patient's photo, find Betamethasone. Click the down arrow next to **Select** and choose **Administer**.
- Follow the Medication Wizard's prompts to administer Gabriela Valenzuela's betamethasone. Select **Yes** when asked whether to document the injection in the MAR.
- When the Wizard stops asking questions, click on **Finish**.
- Now click on **Nurse-Client Interactions**.
- Select and view the video titled **0805: Patient Teaching—Abruption**. (*Note:* Check the virtual clock to see whether enough time has elapsed. You can use the fast-forward feature to advance the time by 2-minute intervals if the video is not yet available. Then click on **Patient Care** and **Nurse-Client Interactions** to refresh the screen.)

13. According to the video, what will help increase the oxygen supply to the baby and prevent further separation of the placenta?

- Click on **Leave the Floor**.
- Click on **Look at Your Preceptor's Evaluation**.
- Click on **Medication Scorecard** and review the evaluation. How did you do? (*Hint:* For a refresher on reading your Medication Scorecard, see the tours in the **Getting Started** section of this workbook.

Exercise 2

Virtual Hospital Activity

30 minutes

- Sign in to work at Pacific View Regional Hospital on the Obstetrics Floor for Period of Care 2. (*Note:* If you are already in the virtual hospital from a previous exercise, click on **Leave the Floor** and then on **Restart the Program** to get to the sign-in window.)
- From the Patient List, select Gabriela Valenzuela (Room 205).
- Click on **Go to Nurses' Station**.
- Click on **Chart** and then on **205**.
- Click on **Diagnostic Reports**.

1. Gabriela Valenzuela had an ultrasound done on Tuesday to determine the source of the bleeding. What were the findings on the ultrasound?

- Click on the **Laboratory Reports**.

2. What were Gabriela Valenzuela's hemoglobin and hematocrit levels on Tuesday? How do these findings compare with Wednesday's report? Has there been a significant change?

3. According to your textbook information, it is important that the patient's hematocrit level be

   maintained above _____.

Review your textbook.

4. What clinical manifestations would indicate a worsening in the condition of either the patient or the fetus?

- Click on **Return to Nurses' Station**.
- Click on **EPR** and **Login**.
- Select **205** from the Patient drop-down menu and **Vital Signs** from the Category drop-down menu.
- Using the blue arrows, scroll to review the vital sign data over the last 12 hours.

5. From 0000 Wednesday until 1200 Wednesday, would you consider Gabriela Valenzuela's condition stable or unstable? State the rationale for your answer.

- Click on **Exit EPR**.
- Click on **205** at the bottom of the screen.
- Click on **Patient Care** and then on **Nurse-Client Interactions**.
- Select and view the video titled **1140: Intervention—Bleeding, Comfort**. (*Note:* Check the virtual clock to see whether enough time has elapsed. You can use the fast-forward feature to advance the time by 2-minute intervals if the video is not yet available. Then click on **Patient Care** and **Nurse-Client Interactions** to refresh the screen.)

6. What happened to elicit this interaction? (*Hint:* Review the Nurse's Notes for Wednesday 1140.)

7. What actions did the nurse take during the video?

Exercise 3

Virtual Hospital Activity

15 minutes

- Sign in to work at Pacific View Regional Hospital on the Obstetrics Floor for Period of Care 3. (*Note*: If you are already in the virtual hospital from a previous exercise, click on **Leave the Floor** and then on **Restart the Program** to get to the sign-in window.)
- From the Patient List, select Gabriela Valenzuela (Room 205).
- Click on **Go to Nurses' Station**.
- Click on **Kardex** and then on tab **205**.

1. What problem areas have been identified by the nurse related to Gabriela Valenzuela's diagnosis?

2. What is the focus of the desired outcomes related to the problems you listed in question 1?

3. List four possible patient problems appropriate for Gabriela Valenzuela at this time.

- Click on **Return to Nurses' Station**.
- Click on **Chart**.
- Click on **205**.
- Click on **Patient Education**.

4. According to the Patient Education sheet in Gabriela Valenzuela's chart, what are the educational goals related to the patient's diagnosis?

- Click on **Nurse's Notes**.

5. What education has been completed by the nurses through Period of Care 3? Include the times and topics discussed.

6. What are some barriers to learning that the nurse may confront with this patient?

7. How can the nurse overcome each of the barriers you identified in the previous question?

Pain Management During Childbirth

Reading Assignments:

McKinney, James, Murray, Nelson, and Ashwill: Maternal-Child Nursing, 5th edition (Chapter 18)

Perry, Hockenberry, Lowdermilk, and Wilson: Maternal Child Nursing Care, 5th edition (Chapter 14)

Patients: Kelly Brady, Room 203
Gabriela Valenzuela, Room 205
Laura Wilson, Room 206

Objectives:

• Assess and identify factors that influence pain perception.
• Describe selected nonpharmacologic and pharmacologic measures for pain management during labor and birth.

Exercise 1

Virtual Hospital Activity

45 minutes

• Sign in to work at Pacific View Regional Hospital on the Obstetrics Floor for Period of Care 1. (*Note:* If you are already in the virtual hospital from a previous exercise, click on **Leave the Floor** and then on **Restart the Program** to get to the sign-in window.)
• From the Patient List, select Laura Wilson (Room 206).
• Click on **Get Report**.

1. What is Laura Wilson's current condition according to the change-of-shift report?

• Click on **Go to Nurses' Station**.
• Click on **206** at the bottom of the screen.
• Read the Initial Observations.

2. What is your impression of Laura Wilson's condition?

- Click on **Patient Care** and then on **Nurse-Client Interactions**.
- Select and view the video titled **0730: Patient Assessment**. (*Note:* Check the virtual clock to see whether enough time has elapsed. You can use the fast-forward feature to advance the time by 2-minute intervals if the video is not yet available. Then click on **Patient Care** and **Nurse-Client Interactions** to refresh the screen.)

3. What is Laura Wilson's assessment of her current condition? How does this compare with the information you received from the shift report and the Initial Observations summary?

- Click on **Chart** and then on **206**.
- Click on **Nursing Admission**.

4. List Laura Wilson's admission diagnoses. (*Hint:* See page 1 of the Nursing Admission form.)

5. What is your perception of Laura Wilson's behavior? What data did you collect during this exercise that led you to this perception?

6. Think about the following questions and then discuss your ideas with your classmates: Do your personal values and beliefs contribute to your perception of Laura Wilson's behavior? If so, how? What nursing interventions might help to overcome your personal biases when dealing with Laura Wilson?

Read about factors influencing pain response in your textbook.

Continue reviewing Laura Wilson's **Nursing Admission** form as needed to answer question 7.

7. Each woman's pain during childbirth is unique and is influenced by a variety of factors. For each factor listed below and on the next page, explain how that factor influences pain perception (in the middle column). In the right column, list data from Laura Wilson's Nursing Admission that support how that factor might relate to her particular pain perception.

Factor	Typical Effect on Pain Perception	Laura Wilson's Supporting Data
Anxiety		

Factor	Typical Effect on Pain Perception	Laura Wilson's Supporting Data
Previous experience		
Religious/Culture		
Support		

Exercise 2

Virtual Hospital Activity

45 minutes

- Sign in to work at Pacific View Regional Hospital on the Obstetrics Floor for Period of Care 2. (*Note*: If you are already in the virtual hospital from a previous exercise, click on **Leave the Floor** and then on **Restart the Program** to get to the sign-in window.)
- From the Patient List, select Gabriela Valenzuela (Room 205).

Now read about pharmacologic pain management for labor in your textbook.

- Click on **Get Report** and review this report.

1. Is Gabriela Valenzuela in labor at this time? Give a rationale for this answer.

- Click on **Go to Nurses' Station**.
- Click on **205** at the bottom of the screen.
- Click on **Patient Care** and then on **Nurse-Client Interactions**.
- Select and view the video titled **1140: Intervention—Bleeding, Comfort**. (*Note:* Check the virtual clock to see whether enough time has elapsed. You can use the fast-forward feature to advance the time by 2-minute intervals if the video is not yet available. Then click on **Patient Care** and **Nurse-Client Interactions** to refresh the screen.)
- After viewing the video, click on **Chart** and then on **205**.
- Click on **Nurse's Notes**.
- Scroll to the entry for 1140 on Wednesday.

2. How is Gabriela Valenzuela tolerating labor at this time?

3. What pain interventions does the nurse implement at this time?

In your textbook, read about fentanyl and about the use of systemic drugs for labor.

4. What is the action of this drug?

Let's begin the process for preparing and administering Gabriela Valenzuela's fentanyl dose.

- First, click on **Return to Room 205** and then on **Medication Room**.
- Next, click on **MAR** and then on tab **205**.
- Scroll down to the PRN Medication Administration Record for Wednesday.

5. What is the ordered dose of fentanyl?

- Click on **Return to Medication Room**.
- Click on **Automated System**.
- Click on **Login**.
- In box 1, click on **Gabriela Valenzuela, 205**.
- In box 2, click on **Automated System Drawer A-F**.
- Click on **Fentanyl citrate**.
- Click on **Put Medication on Tray**.
- Click on **Close Drawer**.
- Click on **View Medication Room**.
- Click on **Preparation**.
- Click on **Prepare** and follow the Preparation Wizard prompts to complete preparation of Gabriela Valenzuela's fentanyl dose. When the Wizard stops requesting information, click **Finish**.
- Click on **Return to Medication Room**.
- Click on **205** to go to the patient's room.

6. What additional assessments must be completed before you administer Gabriela Valenzuela's medication?

7. Why is it important to check Gabriela Valenzuela's respirations before giving the dose of fentanyl?

8. What safety precautions should be in effect for Gabriela Valenzuela after she receives this dose of fentanyl?

- Click on **Patient Care** and then on **Medication Administration**.
- Click on **Review Your Medications** and verify the accuracy of your preparation. Click on **Return to Room 205**.
- Next, click the down arrow next to **Select** and choose **Administer**.
- Follow the Administration Wizard prompts to administer Gabriela Valenzuela's fentanyl dose. (*Note:* Click **Yes** when asked whether to document this administration in the MAR.)
- When the Wizard stops asking questions, click **Finish**.
- Still in Gabriela Valenzuela's room, click on **Patient Care** and then on **Nurse-Client Interactions**.
- Select and view the video titled **1155: Evaluation—Comfort Measures**. (*Note:* Check the virtual clock to see whether enough time has elapsed. You can use the fast-forward feature to advance the time by 2-minute intervals if the video is not yet available. Then click on **Patient Care** and **Nurse-Client Interactions** to refresh the screen.)

9. How effective were the interventions you identified in question 3?

Read about nonpharmacologic interventions in your textbook.

10. Gabriela Valenzuela is most likely experiencing _____. Other symptoms

of hyperventilation include _____.

11. What interventions does the nurse suggest to deal with this problem? List other interventions described in your textbook.

At the end of the 1155 video, Gabriela Valenzuela states that she "doesn't want any needles" in her back. Learn more about this by reading about epidural block in your textbook.

12. What could you tell Gabriela Valenzuela to help her make an informed decision about anesthesia for labor? In the table below, list advantages and disadvantages of epidural anesthesia.

Advantages	Disadvantages

Before leaving this period of care, let's see how you did preparing and administering the patient's medication.

- Click on **Leave the Floor**.
- Click on **Look at Your Preceptor's Evaluation**.
- Click on **Medication Scorecard** and review the evaluation. How did you do? (*Hint:* For a refresher on reading your Medication Scorecard, see the tours in the **Getting Started** section of this workbook.

Exercise 3

Virtual Hospital Activity

20 minutes

Read about general anesthesia in your textbook.

- Sign in to work at Pacific View Regional Hospital on the Obstetrics Floor for Period of Care 4. (*Note*: If you are already in the virtual hospital from a previous exercise, click on **Leave the Floor** and then on **Restart the Program** to get to the sign-in window.)
- From the Nurses' Station, click on **Chart** and then on **203** for Kelly Brady's chart. (*Remember:* You are not able to visit patients or administer medications during Period of Care 4. You are able to review patient records only.)
- Click on **Nurse's Notes**.
- Scroll to the entry for 1730 on Wednesday.

1. Why does the anesthesiologist plan to use general anesthesia during Kelly Brady's cesarean section? (*Hint*: Read the relevant section on contraindications and precautions in your textbook.)

2. Why is Kelly Brady upset about receiving general anesthesia for her surgery?

- Click on **Physician's Orders**.
- Review the entry for Wednesday at 1540.

3. What preoperative medications are ordered for Kelly Brady?

- Click on **Return to Nurses' Station**.
- Click on the **Drug** icon in the lower left corner of your screen to access the Drug Guide.
- Use the search box or the scroll bar to read about each of the drugs you listed in question 3.

4. All of these medications are given preoperatively to help prevent aspiration pneumonia. Using information from the Drug Guide and from the section about general anesthesia in your textbook, match each of the medications below with the description of how it specifically works to prevent aspiration pneumonia.

Medication	How It Prevents Aspiration Pneumonia
_____ Sodium citrate/citric acid (Bicitra)	a. Decreases the production of gastric acid
_____ Metoclopramide (Reglan)	b. Prevents nausea and vomiting and accelerates gastric emptying
_____ Ranitidine (Zantac)	c. Neutralizes acidic stomach contents

5. How would you expect general anesthesia to affect Kelly Brady's baby? Why?

Labor and Birth Complications

Reading Assignments:

McKinney, James, Murray, Nelson, and Ashwill: Maternal-Child Nursing, 5th edition
    (Chapters 19 and 27)
Perry, Hockenberry, Lowdermilk, and Wilson: Maternal Child Nursing Care, 5th edition (Chapter 17)

Patients: Dorothy Grant, Room 201
                Stacey Crider, Room 202
                Kelly Brady, Room 203
                Gabriela Valenzuela, Room 205

Objectives:

- Assess and identify signs and symptoms present in the patient with preterm labor.
- Describe appropriate nursing care for the patient in preterm labor.
- Develop a birth plan to meet the needs of the preterm infant.

Exercise 1

Virtual Hospital Activity

20 minutes

- Sign in to work at Pacific View Regional Hospital on the Obstetrics Floor for Period of Care 2. (*Note:* If you are already in the virtual hospital from a previous exercise, click on **Leave the Floor** and then on **Restart the Program** to get to the sign-in window.)
- From the Patient List, select Dorothy Grant and Gabriela Valenzuela.
- Click on **Go to Nurses' Station**.
- Click on **Chart** and then on **201** for Dorothy Grant's chart.
- Click on **History and Physical**.

1. Using the information found in the History and Physical section, complete the table below for Dorothy Grant.

Patient	Weeks of Gestation	Reason for Admission
Dorothy Grant		

- Click on **Return to Nurses' Station**.
- Now click again on **Chart**; this time, select **205**.
- Click on **History and Physical**.

2. Using the information found in the History and Physical section, complete the table below for Gabriela Valenzuela.

Patient	Weeks of Gestation	Reason for Admission
Gabriela Valenzuela		

- Click on **Return to Nurses' Station**.
- Click on **201** at the bottom of the screen to go to Dorothy Grant's room.
- Click on **Patient Care**.
- Click on **Physical Assessment**.
- Click on **Pelvic** and then on **Reproductive**.

3. Complete the table below with the results of Dorothy Grant's initial cervical examination.

Patient	Time	Dilation	Effacement	Station
Dorothy Grant				

- Click on **Return to Nurses' Station**.
- Click on **205** to go to Gabriela Valenzuela's room.
- Click on **Patient Care**.
- Click on **Physical Assessment**.
- Click on **Pelvic** and then on **Reproductive**.

4. Record the results of Gabriela Valenzuela's initial cervical examination in the table below.

Patient	Time	Dilation	Effacement	Station
Gabriela Valenzuela				

Read about preterm labor in your textbook.

5. Preterm labor is defined as _____

_____.

6. As of Wednesday at 0800, would you consider both these patients to be in preterm labor? Give a rationale for your answer.

Read about tocolytics in your textbook.

7. Match each medication below with the description of how it works as a tocolytic agent. (*Hint:* Letters may be used more than once.)

Medication

_____ Magnesium sulfate

_____ Nifedipine (Procardia)

_____ Ritodrine (Yutopar)

_____ Terbutaline (Brethine)

_____ Indomethacin (Indocin)

Tocolytic Action

a. Blocks calcium from entering smooth muscle cells, thus relaxing uterine contractions

b. Inhibits uterine muscle activity as a result of stimulation of beta-adrenergic receptors of the sympathetic nervous system

c. Exact mechanism unclear, but promotes relaxation of smooth muscles

d. Suppresses preterm labor by inhibiting the synthesis of prostaglandins

Exercise 2

Virtual Hospital Activity

30 minutes

- Sign in to work at Pacific View Regional Hospital on the Obstetrics Floor for Period of Care 1. (*Note*: If you are already in the virtual hospital from a previous exercise, click on **Leave the Floor** and then **Restart the Program** to get to the sign-in window.)
- From the Patient List, select Stacey Crider (Room 202).
- Click on **Get Report**.

Stacey Crider was admitted yesterday in preterm labor and placed on magnesium sulfate. Her other admission diagnoses were bacterial vaginosis and gestational diabetes with poorly controlled blood glucose levels.

1. What is Stacey Crider's current status in regard to preterm labor?

- Click on **Go to Nurses' Station**.
- Click on **Chart** and then on **202**.
- Click on **Physician's Orders**.
- Scroll to the orders for Wednesday at 0715.

2. Which of these orders relate specifically to Stacey Crider's diagnosis of preterm labor?

- Scroll to the orders for Wednesday at 0730.

3. What medication changes are ordered?

Read about terbutaline in your textbook.

4. Why do you think Stacey Crider's physician changed the orders so quickly?

- Click on **Return to Nurses' Station**.
- Click on **202** at the bottom of the screen.
- Inside the patient's room, click on **Take Vital Signs**.

5. What are Stacey Crider's current vital signs?

6. Which of these parameters provides you with the most important information before giving Stacey Crider's nifedipine dose? Why? (*Hint*: Read about nifedipine in your textbook.)

Like Dorothy Grant and Kelly Brady, Stacey Crider is also receiving betamethasone.

Read about betamethasone in your textbook.

7. Why are all three of these patients receiving antenatal glucocorticoid therapy?

8. What other benefit does this class of medication seem to provide for preterm infants?

- Click on **MAR**.
- Click on tab **202**.

9. What is Stacey Crider's prescribed betamethasone dosage?

10. How does this dosage compare with the recommended dosage in your textbook?

- Click on **Return to Nurses' Station**.
- Click on **Medication Room**.
- Click on **Unit Dosage**.
- Click on drawer **202**.
- Click on **Betamethasone**.
- Click on **Put Medication on Tray**.
- Click on **Close Drawer**.
- Click on **View Medication Room**.
- Click on **Preparation**.
- Click on **Prepare** and follow the Preparation Wizard's prompts to complete preparation of Stacey Crider's betamethasone dose.
- Click on **Return to Medication Room**.
- Click on **202** to return to Stacey Crider's room.
- Click on **Check Armband**.
- Click on **Check Allergies**.
- Click on **Patient Care**.
- Click on **Medication Administration**.
- Find Betamethasone listed on the left side of your screen. To its right, click on the down arrow next to **Select** and choose **Administer**.
- Follow the Administration Wizard's prompts to administer Stacey Crider's betamethasone injection. Indicate **Yes** to document the injection in the MAR.
- Click on **Leave the Floor**.
- Click on **Look at Your Preceptor's Evaluation**.
- Click on **Medication Scorecard**. How did you do?

Exercise 3

Virtual Hospital Activity

30 minutes

- Sign in to work at Pacific View Regional Hospital on the Obstetrics Floor for Period of Care 4. (*Note:* If you are already in the virtual hospital from a previous exercise, click on **Leave the Floor** and then on **Restart the Program** to get to the sign-in window.)
- From the Nurses' Station, click on **Chart**. (*Remember:* You are not able to visit patients or administer medications during Period of Care 4. You are able to review patient records only.)
- Click on **201** for Dorothy Grant's chart.
- Click on **Nurse's Notes**.
- Scroll to the note for Wednesday 1815.

  1. What are the findings from Dorothy Grant's cervical examination at this time?

- Scroll to the note for Wednesday 1840. It states that Dorothy Grant is being prepped for delivery.

  2. If you were the nurse caring for Dorothy Grant during delivery, what special preparations would you make to care for the baby immediately after birth?

- Click on **Return to Nurses' Station**.
- Click again on **Chart**, but this time choose **205** for Gabriela Valenzuela's chart.
- Click on **Physician's Notes** and scroll to the note for Wednesday 0800.

  3. What is the anticipated outcome of Gabriela Valenzuela's labor, according to this note?

• Scroll to the notes for Wednesday 1415 and 1455.

4. What preparations have been made during the day for the birth of Gabriela Valenzuela's baby?

Read the information on cesarean birth found in your textbook.

• Click on **Return to Nurses' Station**.
• Click on **Chart** and then on **203**.
• Click on **Physician's Notes**.
• Scroll to the note for Wednesday 1530.

Kelly Brady was admitted yesterday with severe preeclampsia at 26 weeks of gestation. Her preeclampsia is now worsening.

5. Why does her physician now recommend immediate delivery?

6. What general risks related to cesarean section does Kelly Brady's physician discuss with her?

7. Because of Kelly Brady's early gestational age (26 weeks), her physician anticipates a classical uterine incision. How will this type of incision affect Kelly Brady's birth options in future pregnancies?

• Click on **Physician's Orders** and scroll to the orders for Wednesday 1540.

8. List the orders to be carried out prior to Kelly Brady's surgery. State the purpose of each.

Order	Purpose

9. Can you think of other common preoperative procedures? List them below. (*Hint*: Refer to a basic Medical-Surgical textbook for ideas if you need help!)

Medication Administration

Reading Assignments:

McKinney, James, Murray, Nelson, and Ashwill: Maternal-Child Nursing, 5th edition
   (Chapters 25, 26, and 27)
Perry, Hockenberry, Lowdermilk, and Wilson: Maternal Child Nursing Care, 5th edition
   (Chapters 12, 17, and 25)

Patients: Dorothy Grant, Room 201
   Stacey Crider, Room 202
   Maggie Gardner, Room 204
   Laura Wilson, Room 206

Objective:

• Correctly administer selected medications to obstetric patients, observing the six rights.

Exercise 1

Virtual Hospital Activity

30 minutes

Dorothy Grant was admitted at 30 weeks of gestation for observation following blunt abdominal trauma (she was kicked in the abdomen). She is bleeding vaginally and may have sustained a placental abruption. Your assignment is to give Rho(D) immune globulin to her.

• Sign in to work at Pacific View Regional Hospital on the Obstetrics Floor for Period of Care 2. (*Note*: If you are already in the virtual hospital from a previous exercise, click on **Leave the Floor** and then on **Restart the Program** to get to the sign-in window.)
• From the Patient List, select Dorothy Grant (Room 201).

Read about Rho(D) immune globulin in your textbook.

1. Explain why Rho(D) immune globulin is given and provide the rationale.

2. All of the following are reasons that Rho(D) immune globulin might be administered. Select the reason it has been ordered for Dorothy Grant.

    _____ Within 72 hours of giving birth to an Rh-positive infant

    _____ Prophylactically at 28 weeks of gestation

    _____ Following an incident or exposure risk that occurs after 28 weeks of gestation

    _____ During first trimester pregnancy following miscarriage or elective abortion or ectopic pregnancy

3. List the information about Dorothy Grant that must be determined before giving her Rho(D) immune globulin.

• Click on **Go to Nurses' Station**.
• Click on **Chart** and then on **201**.
• Click on **Physician's Orders** and scroll to the orders for Wednesday 0730.

4. Write the physician's order for Rho(D) immune globulin.

5. According to your textbook, is this the correct dosage and route? (*Hint:* Read about postpartum management in your textbook.)

- Click on **Laboratory Reports**
- Locate the results for 0245 Wednesday.
- Scroll down to find the type and screen results.

6. Dorothy Grant's blood type is _____.

7. What additional information do you need? Why? Is that information available?

- Click on **Return to Nurses' Station**.
- Click on **Medication Room**.
- Click on **Refrigerator**; then click on the refrigerator door to open it.
- Click on **Put Medication on Tray**.
- Click on **Close Door**.
- Click on **View Medication Room**.
- Click on **Preparation**.
- Click on **Prepare** and follow the prompts to complete preparation of this medication.
- Click on **Return to Medication Room**.
- Click on **201** to go to Dorothy Grant's room.
- Click on **Check Armband**.
- Click on **Patient Care**.
- Click on **Medication Administration**.

You are almost ready to give Dorothy Grant's injection. However, before you do . . .

8. Rho(D) immune globulin is often considered a blood product.
   a. True
   b. False

9. Suppose Dorothy Grant absolutely refuses to accept blood or blood products because of her religious beliefs. How would you handle the situation?

Now you're ready to administer the medication!

- Click on the down arrow next to **Select**; choose **Administer**.
- Follow the prompts to administer Dorothy Grant's injection. Indicate **Yes** to document the injection in the MAR.
- Click on **Leave the Floor**.
- Click on **Look at Your Preceptor's Evaluation**.
- Click on **Medication Scorecard**. How did you do?

Exercise 2

Virtual Hospital Activity

20 minutes

- Sign in to work at Pacific View Regional Hospital on the Obstetrics Floor for Period of Care 1. (*Note*: If you are already in the virtual hospital from a previous exercise, click on **Leave the Floor** and then on **Restart the Program** to get to the sign-in window.)
- From the Patient List, select Maggie Gardner (Room 204).
- Click on **Go to Nurses' Station**.
- Click on the **Chart** and then on **204**.
- Click on the **Nursing Admission**.

1. Maggie Gardner verbalizes anxiety repeatedly throughout the Nursing Admission. What is her primary concern? Why? Provide documentation.

2. Maggie Gardner states that before this pregnancy she had a highly adaptive coping mechanism. How does she consider her ability to cope at this point? Why? (*Hint*: See the Coping and Stress Tolerance section in the Nursing Admission.)

- Click on the **Physician's Orders**.

3. What medication has the physician ordered to help Maggie Gardner with her anxiety?

- Click on **Return to Nurses' Station**.
- Click on the **Drug** icon in the lower-left corner of your screen.
- Use the search box or the scroll bar to find the medication you identified in question 3.
- Review all of the information provided regarding this drug.

4. What is the drug's mechanism of action?

- Click on **Return to Nurses' Station**.
- Click on **204** to go to Maggie Gardner's room.
- Click on **Patient Care** and then on **Nurse-Client Interactions**.
- Select and view the video titled **0745: Evaluation—Efficacy of Drugs**. (*Note:* Check the virtual clock to see whether enough time has elapsed. You can use the fast-forward feature to advance the time by 2-minute intervals if the video is not yet available. Then click on **Patient Care** and **Nurse-Client Interactions** to refresh the screen.)

5. According to the nurse, how long will it take for Maggie Gardner to see therapeutic effects of the medication that has been ordered? How does this correlate with what you learned in the teaching section of the Drug Guide?

Exercise 3

Virtual Hospital Activity

15 minutes

In this exercise, you will administer betamethasone to Stacey Crider, who was admitted to the hospital at 27 weeks of gestation in preterm labor.

- Sign in to work at Pacific View Regional Hospital on the Obstetrics Floor for Period of Care 1. (*Note*: If you are already in the virtual hospital from a previous exercise, click on **Leave the Floor** and then on **Restart the Program** to get to the sign-in window.)
- From the Patient List, select Stacey Crider (Room 202).

1. Before preparing Stacey Crider's betamethasone, what do you need to do first?

- Click on **Go to Nurses' Station**.
- Click on **Chart** and then on **202**.
- Click on **Physician's Orders**.
- Scroll until you find the order for betamethasone.

2. After verifying the physician's order, what is your next step?

- Click on **Return to Nurses' Station**.
- Click on **Medication Room**.
- Click on **Unit Dosage**.
- Click on drawer **202**.
- Click on **Betamethasone**.
- Click on **Put Medication on Tray**.
- Click on **Close Drawer**.
- Click on **View Medication Room**.
- Click on **Preparation**.
- Click on **Prepare** and follow the prompts to complete preparation of Stacey Crider's betamethasone dose.
- Click on **Return to Medication Room**.

3. Now that the medication is prepared, what is your next step?

- Click on **202** to go to the patient's room.
- Click on **Check Armband**.
- Click on **Check Allergies**.
- Click on **Patient Care**.
- Click on **Medication Administration**.
- Click on the down arrow next to **Select** and choose **Administer**.
- Follow the prompts to administer Stacey Crider's betamethasone injection.

4. What is the final step in the process?

- If you haven't already done so, indicate **Yes** to document the injection in the MAR.
- Click on **Leave the Floor**.
- Click on **Look at Your Preceptor's Evaluation**.
- Click on **Medication Scorecard**. How did you do?

Exercise 4

Virtual Hospital Activity

30 minutes

- Sign in to work at Pacific View Regional Hospital on the Obstetrics Floor for Period of Care 1. (*Note*: If you are already in the virtual hospital from a previous exercise, click on **Leave the Floor** and then on **Restart the Program** to get to the sign-in window.)
- From the Patient List, select Laura Wilson (Room 206).
- Click on **Go to Nurses' Station**.
- Click on **MAR**.
- Click on the tab for **206**.

1. Laura Wilson's medications for Wednesday include several different types of drugs. In the list below, select the one that is used to treat her HIV-positive status.

   _____ Zidovudine 200 mg PO every 8 hours

   _____ Prenatal multivitamin 1 tablet PO daily

   _____ Lactated Ringer's 1000 mL IV continuous

- Click on **Return to Nurses' Station**.
- Click on the **Drug** icon in the lower-left corner of the screen.
- Using the search box or the scroll bar, find the drug you identified in question 1.

2. What is the drug's mechanism of action?

3. What is the drug's therapeutic effect?

4. Does this medication cross the placenta, or is it distributed in breast milk?

5. What symptoms/side effects of this medication need to be reported to the physician?

6. How should this medication be taken?

7. Your final assignment dealing with obstetric patients is to give Laura Wilson the medication that is due at 0800. During these lessons, we have provided you with the detailed instructions on how to give medications. Now it is time for you to try this on your own. Don't forget the six rights of medication administration. Document below how you did.

If you'd like to get more practice, there are other medications that can be given at the beginning of the first three periods of care. Below is a list of the patients, the medications, the routes of administration, and the administration times you can use. As you practice, be sure to select the correct patient when you sign in. That way, you can get a Medication Scorecard for evaluation after you prepare and administer a medication. (*Remember:* If you need help at any time, refer to the tours in the **Getting Started** section of this workbook.)

PERIOD OF CARE 1

Room 201, Dorothy Grant

0730/0800—Betamethasone 12 mg IM

Prenatal multivitamin PO

Room 202, Stacey Crider

0800—Prenatal multivitamin PO

Metronidazole 500 mg PO

Betamethasone 12 mg IM

Insulin lispro subQ

Nifedipine 20 mg PO

Room 203, Kelly Brady

0730/0800—Prenatal multivitamin PO

Ferrous sulfate PO

Labetalol hydrochloride 400 mg PO

Nifedipine 10 mg PO

Room 204, Maggie Gardner

0800—Prenatal multivitamin PO

Buspirone hydrochloride 5 mg PO

Room 205, Gabriela Valenzuela

0800—Ampicillin 2 g IV

Betamethasone 12 mg IM

Prenatal multivitamin PO

Room 206, Laura Wilson

0800—Zidovudine 200 mg PO

Prenatal multivitamin PO

PERIOD OF CARE 2

Room 201, Dorothy Grant

1200—Rho(D) immune globulin IM

Room 202, Stacey Crider

1200—Insulin lispro subQ

Room 203, Kelly Brady

1130—Betamethasone 12 mg IM

Room 204, Maggie Gardner

1115—Prednisone 40 mg PO

Aspirin 81 mg PO

PERIOD OF CARE 3

Room 204, Maggie Gardner

1500—Buspirone 5 mg PO

Support for Families Experiencing the Loss of a Newborn

Reading Assignments:

McKinney, James, Murray, Nelson, and Ashwill: Maternal-Child Nursing, 5th edition (Chapter 24)

Perry, Hockenberry, Lowdermilk, and Wilson: Maternal Child Nursing Care, 5th edition
(Chapters 25 and 36)

Patient: Maggie Gardner, Room 204

Objectives:

- Identify the various types of loss as they relate to a pregnancy.
- Describe the stages and phases of the grieving process.
- Identify various methods of coping exhibited by patients who have experienced the loss of a newborn.

Exercise 1

Writing Activity

15 minutes

1. Parents may grieve not only the death of a newborn, but also the birth of a baby with a

   _____ or _____.

2. At what other times might couples grieve a loss related to pregnancy? (*Hint:* Consider various readings
   you have completed.)

3. Women experience what type of effects if a pregnancy ends early because of miscarriage?

4. Parents need to be given the opportunity to "parent" the infant in any manner they wish or are able to before and after death.
   a. True
   b. False

5. All women and men who undergo a loss receive the support that they need.
   a. True
   b. False

6. NICU nurses feel helpless and sorrowful. This type of grief must be allowed. Do you agree? Why or why not?

Exercise 2

Virtual Hospital Activity

10 minutes

- Sign in to work at Pacific View Regional Hospital on the Obstetrics Floor for Period of Care 4. (*Note:* If you are already in the virtual hospital from a previous exercise, click on **Leave the Floor** and then on **Restart the Program** to get to the sign-in window.)
- Click on **Chart** and then on **204** for Maggie Gardner's chart. (*Remember:* You are not able to visit patients or administer medications during Period of Care 4. You are able to review patient records only.)
- Review the **History and Physical**.

1. How many losses related to pregnancy has Maggie Gardner experienced?

- Click on the **Nursing Admission**.

2. What is the first evidence you find that Maggie Gardner's previous losses are affecting her current pregnancy and care? (*Hint*: Review the first five sections.)

- Click on the **Consultations** tab.

3. To what does Maggie Gardner attribute her inability to have a child?

4. List three therapeutic measures the chaplain can use to assist her through these feelings as part of her grieving process.

5. What did the chaplain accomplish during his time with Maggie Gardner?

Exercise 3

Virtual Hospital Activity

15 minutes

Read about grief and loss in your textbook.

1. The grief response is closely linked to the _____ of the mother or father who has experienced the loss.

2. What are the four tasks of grief? (*Hint:* Consider Kübler-Ross theory.)

3. What are the three phases of grief?

4. List some physical symptoms that may manifest during the grieving process.

5. What response typically emerges during intense grief? Why?

6. List three other emotions that are experienced during the time period of intense grief.

7. During the phase of reorganization, what is the most common question? Explain.

- Sign in to work at Pacific View Regional Hospital on the Obstetrics Floor for Period of Care 4. (*Note:* If you are already in the virtual hospital from a previous exercise, click on **Leave the Floor** and then on **Restart the Program** to get to the sign-in window.)
- Click on **Chart** and then on **204**. (*Remember:* You are not able to visit patients or administer medications during Period of Care 4. You are able to review patient records only.)
- Review the **History and Physical**.

8. You have now reviewed Maggie Gardner's History and Physical and compared her information with your textbook's discussion of what happens during the reorganization phase. What correlation do you see?

- Click on **Consultations**.
- Scroll down to review the Pastoral Care Spiritual Assessment.

9. Culture and religion play very large roles in how individuals handle a loss. How has Maggie Gardner handled her losses? (*Hint*: See the Spirituality/Faith Factors section of this consult.)

Care of the Infant with Respiratory Disorders

Reading Assignments:

McKinney, James, Murray, Nelson, and Ashwill: *Maternal-Child Nursing*, 5th edition
    (Chapters 6, 37, and 45)
Perry, Hockenberry, Lowdermilk, and Wilson: *Maternal Child Nursing Care*, 5th edition
    (Chapters 29, 39, and 40)

Patient: Carrie Richards, Room 303

Objectives:

- Discuss etiology and pathophysiology of respiratory syncytial virus (RSV)/bronchiolitis.
- Relate the effect of an infant's level of growth and development on RSV/bronchiolitis.
- Complete a respiratory assessment on an infant and discuss nursing care issues.
- Use the nursing process to develop a nursing care plan for an infant with RSV/bronchiolitis.

Exercise 1

Virtual Hospital Activity

20 minutes

- Sign in to work at Pacific View Regional Hospital on the Pediatrics Floor for Period of Care 1. (*Note:* If you are already in the virtual hospital from a previous exercise, click on **Leave the Floor** and then on **Restart the Program** to get to the sign-in window.)
- From the Patient List, select Carrie Richards (Room 303).
- Click on **Get Report**.
- Click on **Go to Nurses' Station**.
- Click on **Chart** and then on **303**.
- Click on and review the **Emergency Department** records.

- Click on and review the **History and Physical**.
- Click on and review the **Nursing Admission** and the **Physician's Orders** for Tuesday 1700 and 2300.

1. Briefly summarize Carrie's health history since birth.

2. Is Carrie's immunization status current? If not, list the immunization(s) she should receive as soon as possible.

3. Based on Carrie's present respiratory illness, what immunization should she receive when she is 6 months old that may help protect her from further serious respiratory illnesses?

- Before leaving the chart, record Carrie's physical assessment findings on admission in the middle column of the table in question 4. (*Hint:* You can find these in the Emergency Department record.)
- Click on **Return to Nurses' Station**.
- Click on **303** to go to Carrie's room.
- Click on **Patient Care** and then **Physical Assessment**.
- Perform a focused assessment by selecting the various body areas (yellow boxes) and system subcategories (green boxes) as needed to complete question 4.

4. Record your findings from the physical assessment in the far-right column below. Then compare these current findings with those obtained on admission to the ED.

Findings	Admission 1700 Tuesday	Current Findings
Respiratory effort		
Breath sounds		
Adventitious lung sounds		
Sensory/activity level		
Capillary refill		
Pulses		
Supplemental oxygen		

- Still in Carrie's room, click on **Patient Care** and then **Nurse-Client Interactions**.
- Select and view the video titled **0730: Patient Assessment**. (*Note:* Check the virtual clock to see whether enough time has elapsed. You can use the fast-forward feature to advance the time by 2-minute intervals if the video is not yet available. Then click on **Patient Care** and **Nurse-Client Interactions** to refresh the screen.)

5. How does the nurse assess Carrie's respiratory status in the video?

6. Carrie is 3½ months old. At this age, breathing is primarily:
   a. abdominal.
   b. diaphragmatic.

- Click on **Take Vital Signs**.

7. Record Carrie's vital sign results below.

Temperature

Heart rate

Respiratory rate

Oxygen saturation

Blood pressure

8. Based on Carrie's current physical assessment findings and vital signs, what conclusion might be drawn about her respiratory status and general health at this time?

- Click on **EPR** and **Login**.
- Select **303** as the patient's room.
- Choose various categories as needed to record Carrie's vital signs and physical assessment findings in the EPR. Be sure to include respiratory findings and IV status.

Exercise 2

Writing Activity

15 minutes

1. What is RSV/bronchiolitis? Briefly describe the characteristic progression of this illness in children. Also identify any associated clinical manifestations.

2. How is this illness transmitted?

3. Describe the steps that can be taken to reduce or prevent the transmission of this illness.

4. List four priority nursing interventions for an infant with RSV/bronchiolitis.

5. What prophylactic medication is given to prevent RSV/bronchiolitis?

   a. How is this medication administered?

   b. When should this medication be administered?

   c. Given Carrie's history of birth and current illness, describe her status as a candidate to receive this prophylactic medication. Provide a rationale. (*Hint:* See History and Physical.)

Exercise 3

Virtual Hospital Activity

45 minutes

- Sign in to work at Pacific View Regional Hospital on the Pediatrics Floor for Period of Care 1. (*Note:* If you are already in the virtual hospital from a previous exercise, click on **Leave the Floor** and then on **Restart the Program** to get to the sign-in window.)
- From the Patient List, select Carrie Richards (Room 303).
- Click on **Go to Nurses' Station**.
- Click on **Chart** and then on **303** for Carrie's chart.
- Click on **Emergency Department** and review this record.

1. What are Carrie's vital signs on admission to the ED at 1630? Which findings are out of normal range for a child her age?

2. Briefly describe the findings for Carrie recorded in the ED Systems Review and in the ED Nurse's Notes at 1800. Put an asterisk next to any findings that are abnormal for a child Carrie's age.

3. List the five cardinal clinical signs of respiratory distress (RD) in an infant.

- Still in the Emergency Department section of the chart, compare the findings in the ED Nurse's Notes at 1800 and 1900.

4. What clinical signs documented by the nurse indicate a change in Carrie's respiratory status at 1900?

5. What specific intervention is performed to improve Carrie's oxygenation status?

6. What medication is administered to Carrie to improve her respiratory status in the ED?

7. Describe the intended effect of this medication in a child with RSV/bronchiolitis who is wheezing and has a lower airway infection.

8. Describe how this medication is administered in an infant Carrie's age. What is the rationale for this method of administration? (*Hint:* Refer to the Drug Guide.)

9. List two side effects of this medication for which the nurses should be vigilant.

10. Identify priority nursing assessments that need to be performed after the nebulizer treatment is given.

11. What is the primary medical diagnosis listed for Carrie?

12. List two interventions for Carrie based on your review of her status in the ED.

13. In the 1800 ED Nurse's Notes, an important clue is given in relation to the severity of Carrie's status. What might lead you to conclude that her condition is poor? (*Hint:* Consider her age and developmental status.)

- Still in Carrie's chart, click on **Laboratory Reports**.

14. Below, fill in Carrie's laboratory values recorded in the ED at 1800 on Tuesday.

Chemistry	Arterial Blood Gas
Glucose	pH
Sodium (serum)	PaO_2
Potassium	$PaCO_2$
Chloride	Oxygen sat
CO_2 (serum)	
Creatinine	
BUN	
Calcium	

Urinalysis	Hematology
Color	WBC
Clarity	RBC
Glucose	Hgb
Bilirubin	Hct
Blood platelets	
Spec gravity	Differential
pH	Segs
Protein	Bands
Ketones	Lymphocytes
WBC	Monocytes
	Eosinophils
	Basophils

15. Which lab values in the table in question 14 are out of normal range for a child Carrie's age? (*Hint:* Read about common laboratory tests in your textbook.)

• Click on **Emergency Department**. Once again, review the ED Nurse's Notes for 1900 on Tuesday.

16. How is Carrie's respiratory status described? What interventions other than the nebulized medication administration and oxygen were performed to improve Carrie's respiratory status? State the rationale for the intervention performed.

• Still in Carrie's chart, click on and review the **Nursing Admission** and **History and Physical**.

17. List two modifiable health-related risk factors that place Carrie at high risk for the development of RSV/bronchiolitis.

18. List two socioeconomic factors that place Carrie at high risk for the development of RSV/bronchiolitis.

Exercise 4

Virtual Hospital Activity

45 minutes

- Sign in to work at Pacific View Regional Hospital on the Pediatrics Floor for Period of Care 3. (*Note:* If you are already in the virtual hospital from a previous exercise, click on **Leave the Floor** and then on **Restart the Program** to get to the sign-in window.)
- From the Patient List, select Carrie Richards (Room 303).
- Click on **Go to Nurses' Station**.
- Click on **Chart** and then on **303**.
- Review the **Nurse's Notes**.
- Click on **Return to Nurses' Station**.
- Click on **EPR** and then **Login**.
- Select **303** as the patient and **Respiratory** as the category.

1. Summarize Carrie's respiratory status at 1300 on Wednesday based on the 1240 Nurse's Notes and 1215 respiratory assessment data in the EPR.

- Still in the EPR, change the category to **Vital Signs**.

2. What is Carrie's body temperature at 1445?

- Click on **Exit EPR**.
- Click on **MAR** and then on tab **303**.

3. What medication does Carrie have ordered for fever or irritability?

Now let's go to the Medication Room and prepare to administer all of the 1500 medications ordered for Carrie.

- First, click on **Return to Nurses' Station**.
- Next, click on **Medication Room**.
- Click on **MAR** to determine what medications Carrie should receive for 1500. You may review the MAR at any time to verify the correct medication order. (*Hint:* Remember to look at the patient name on the MAR to make sure you have the correct record—you must click on the tab with Carrie's room number within the MAR.) Click on **Return to Medication Room** after reviewing the correct MAR.
- Click on **Unit Dosage** and then on drawer **303**.
- Select the medications you would like to administer. For each medication you select, click on **Put Medication on Tray**. When you are finished, click on **Close Drawer**.
- Click **View Medication Room**.
- Now click on **Automated System** and **Login**.
- Select the correct patient and drawer according to the medication you want to administer. (*Hint:* This automated system is for controlled substances only.) Then click **Open Drawer**.
- Select the medication you would like to administer, click on **Put Medication on Tray**, and then click **Close Drawer**.
- Click **View Medication Room**.
- Click on **Preparation** and select the medication to administer.
- Click **Prepare** and wait for the Preparation Wizard to appear. If the Wizard requests information, provide your answer(s) and then click **Next**.
- Choose the correct patient and then click **Finish**.
- Repeat the previous three steps until all medications that you want to administer are prepared.
- You can click on **Review Your Medications** and then click **Return to Medication Room** when ready. When back in the Medication Room, go directly to Carrie's room by clicking on **303** at the bottom of the screen.
- In Carrie's room, administer the medications, utilizing the rights of medication administration. After you have collected the appropriate assessment data and are ready for administration, click **Patient Care** and then **Medication Administration**. Verify that the correct patient and medication(s) appear in the left-hand window. Then click the down arrow next to Select. From the drop-down menu, select **Administer** and complete the Administration Wizard by providing any information requested. When the Wizard stops asking for information, click **Administer to Patient**. Specify **Yes** when asked whether this administration should be recorded in the MAR. Finally, click **Finish**. Complete these steps for each medication you wish to administer.

Now let's see how you did!

- Click on **Leave the Floor** at the bottom of your screen. From the Floor Menu, select **Look at Your Preceptor's Evaluation**. Then click on **Medication Scorecard**.
- Review the scorecard to see whether or not you correctly administered the appropriate medication(s). If not, why do you think you were incorrect? According to Table C in this scorecard, what resources should be used and what important assessments should be completed before administering the medication(s)? Did you utilize these resources and perform these assessments correctly?

- Print a copy of the Medication Scorecard for your instructor to evaluate.

4. How does the nurse evaluate pain or discomfort in an infant Carrie's age? (*Hint:* See Pain Assessment in your textbook.)

5. What is the most appropriate behavioral pain scale to assess Carrie's pain?

- Still in Carrie's room, click on **Patient Care** and then **Nurse-Client Interactions**.
- Select and view the video titled **1500: Teaching—Oral Medication**. (*Note:* Check the virtual clock to see whether enough time has elapsed. You can use the fast-forward feature to advance the time by 2-minute intervals if the video is not yet available. Then click on **Patient Care** and **Nurse-Client Interactions** to refresh the screen.)

6. How does the nurse teach Carrie's mother to administer the oral medication?

7. What statement(s) does Carrie's mother make about Carrie's eating habits in the last few days prior to admission?

8. What interrelated factors should the nurse consider when an infant has a compromising respiratory illness, such as RSV/bronchiolitis, and the infant's food intake is decreased?

9. What are the implications of these findings for an infant in relation to hydration status and present illness?

10. An infant's illness and hospitalization may represent a significant stressor for a single mother and her infant. What can the nursing staff do to minimize Brenda's anxiety about Carrie's hospitalization?

Care of the Child with Diabetes Mellitus

Reading Assignments:

McKinney, James, Murray, Nelson, and Ashwill: Maternal-Child Nursing, 5th edition
(Chapters 8 and 51)

Perry, Hockenberry, Lowdermilk, and Wilson: Maternal Child Nursing Care, 5th edition
(Chapters 34 and 46)

Patient: George Gonzalez, Room 301

Objectives:

• Discuss the pathophysiology of DM and diabetic ketoacidosis (DKA).

• Compare and contrast type 1 and type 2 DM.

• Discuss management and nursing responsibilities for insulin therapy, diet, exercise, and blood glucose monitoring.

• Contrast causes, signs, and management of hypoglycemia and hyperglycemia.

• Discuss the impact of growth and development on diabetes.

• Identify learning needs of a child (and his family) newly diagnosed with diabetes.

• Develop a plan for teaching a child independence with care of diabetes.

Exercise 1

Virtual Hospital Activity

30 minutes

• Sign in to work at Pacific View Regional Hospital on the Pediatrics Floor for Period of Care 1. (*Note:* If you are already in the virtual hospital from a previous exercise, click on **Leave the Floor** and then on **Restart the Program** to get to the sign-in window.)

• From the Patient List, select George Gonzalez.

• Click on **Go to Nurses' Station**.

• Click on **Chart** and then on **301**.

• Click on **Emergency Department** and review this record.

1. George Gonzalez has been admitted with a diagnosis of DKA. What does this mean? What are the signs of DKA?

2. Based on your textbook and George Gonzalez's chart, what makes George at particular risk for developing diabetes?

3. Match the following to show your understanding of the differences between type 1 and type 2 DM.

Characteristic	**Type of DM**
_____ This is the most common childhood endocrine disease.	a. Type 1
_____ This type results from autoimmune process disorder.	b. Type 2
_____ Cells are unable to use insulin.	
_____ Genetic predisposition is a factor.	
_____ The pancreas is unable to produce insulin.	
_____ Obesity commonly coexists with this type.	

4. What was George Gonzalez's condition like when he was admitted? Was there a precipitating factor?

5. In George Gonzalez's situation upon admission, what type of insulin is used and why? Identify any nursing concerns with the administration of insulin IV.

6. What are the signs of hyperglycemia?

7. What are the signs of hypoglycemia?

8. What was George Gonzalez's blood glucose result on admission?

9. List the normal blood glucose values for a child George Gonzalez's age.

10. What ongoing assessments need to be made? (Focus on the admission diagnosis.)

- Click on **Diagnostic Reports** and review the record.

11. What is HbA_{1C}? Explain its use as a diagnostic tool. How does the normal HbA_{1C} compare with George Gonzalez's labs?

Exercise 2

Virtual Hospital Activity

30 minutes

- Sign in to work at Pacific View Regional Hospital on the Pediatrics Floor for Period of Care 1. (*Note:* If you are already in the virtual hospital from a previous exercise, click on **Leave the Floor** and then on **Restart the Program** to get to the sign-in window.)
- From the Patient List, select George Gonzalez.
- Click on **Go to Nurses' Station**.
- Click on **301** at the bottom of the screen.
- Click on **Patient Care** and then on **Nurse-Client Interactions**.
- Select and view the video titled **0730: Supervision—Glucose Testing**. (*Note*: Check the virtual clock to see whether enough time has elapsed. You can use the fast-forward feature to advance the time by 2-minute intervals if the video is not yet available. Then click again on **Patient Care** and **Nurse-Client Interactions** to refresh the screen.)

1. What did the nurse do that facilitated George Gonzalez's honesty about his testing behavior and how he feels about it?

2. What is the nurse trying to accomplish when she asks George Gonzalez to do his own finger stick? How does his developmental stage affect his compliance with treatment?

3. What are some reasons why George Gonzalez may be noncompliant with blood glucose testing?

- Select and view the video titled **0745: Self-Administering Insulin**. (*Note*: Check the virtual clock to see whether enough time has elapsed. You can use the fast-forward feature to advance the time by 2-minute intervals if the video is not yet available. Then click again on **Patient Care** and **Nurse-Client Interactions** to refresh the screen.)

4. What does the nurse do that is positive as she observes George Gonzalez give his injection?

5. Explain the content and methods you would use in teaching the skill of self-administration of insulin.

6. What are possible barriers to learning the skill of injection technique?

7. List areas of content associated with discussing site rotations.

8. The _____ is the site from which insulin is most rapidly absorbed.

George Gonzalez needs insulin. Complete the following questions before going to the Medication Room.

9. Match each type of insulin with its corresponding characteristics.

Characteristic	Type of Insulin
_____ Onset of 30-60 minutes	a. Regular
_____ Onset of 2-4 hours	b. NPH
_____ Peak at 4-10 hours	
_____ Peak at 2-3 hours	
_____ Duration of 5-8 hours	
_____ Duration of 10-16 hours	

10. At what point during the day is George Gonzalez most at risk for a hypoglycemic reaction?

- Click on **Chart** and then on **301**.
- Click on **Physician's Orders**. Find the order for George Gonzalez's morning dose of insulin.

11. Using George Gonzalez's morning insulin order, describe the steps for drawing up two forms of insulin in one syringe.

12. Why is the short-acting insulin always drawn up first?

Before going to the Medication Room, complete any necessary assessments.

- Click on **MAR** to check the order for insulin; then click on **Return to Room 301**.
- Click on **Medication Room**.
- Using the six rights, prepare the correct dose of insulin for George Gonzalez. When you have prepared the medication, return to George's room and administer it, again following the six rights. (*Hint:* Try to perform these steps on your own. If you need help, refer to **Reducing Medication Errors** in the **Getting Started** section of this workbook.)
- After administering the insulin, click on **Leave the Floor** and then on **Look at Your Preceptor's Evaluations**.
- Next, click on **Medication Scorecard** and review the feedback. How did you do?

Exercise 3

Virtual Hospital Activity

30 minutes

- Sign in to work at Pacific View Regional Hospital on the Pediatrics Floor for Period of Care 2. (*Note:* If you are already in the virtual hospital from a previous exercise, click on **Leave the Floor** and then on **Restart the Program** to get to the sign-in window.)
- From the Patient List, select George Gonzalez.
- Click on **Go to Nurses' Station** and then **301**.

1. List the learning needs of a patient newly diagnosed with diabetes. (*Hint:* Consult your textbook.)

2. Which of the above learning needs apply directly to George Gonzalez and his family?

3. What anticipatory guidance can you offer George Gonzalez's mother with regard to how insulin needs change as he moves toward adolescence?

4. Discuss the relationship among insulin, food, and exercise. Explain it in terms that would be understandable for George Gonzalez and his family.

5. Did you consider the "honeymoon phase" as part of your discussion? Why is this significant to parent teaching? What should you say about it?

- Click on **Patient Care** and then on **Nurse-Client Interactions**.
- Select and view the video titled **1115: Teaching—Disease Process**. (*Note*: Check the virtual clock to see whether enough time has elapsed. You can use the fast-forward feature to advance the time by 2-minute intervals if the video is not yet available. Then click again on **Patient Care** and **Nurse-Client Interactions** to refresh the screen.)

6. What are the sequelae of untreated or poorly managed diabetes? Explain why they occur.

7. Evaluate George Gonzalez's understanding of his condition and management of hypoglycemia.

8. George Gonzalez's mother seems to have a _____ understanding of George's condition and the management of hypoglycemia.

9. Given the responses of George Gonzalez and his mother, is there a need for teaching in this area? If so, what teaching techniques would be most effective?

LESSON 16

Care of the Child with Meningitis

Reading Assignments:

McKinney, James, Murray, Nelson, and Ashwill: Maternal-Child Nursing, 5th edition
(Chapters 7, 39, and 52)

Perry, Hockenberry, Lowdermilk, and Wilson: Maternal Child Nursing Care, 5th edition
(Chapters 29 and 45)

Patient: Stephanie Brown, Room 304

Objectives:

- Describe the pathophysiology of meningitis.
- Discuss risk factors for meningitis.
- Analyze laboratory findings associated with childhood meningitis.
- List assessment data indicative of meningitis.
- Describe the components of a neurologic assessment for a child who is diagnosed with meningitis.
- Explain the rationale for the treatment of meningitis.
- Discuss strategies for supporting a parent and child through diagnosis and treatment.

Exercise 1

Virtual Hospital Activity

30 minutes

- Sign in to work at Pacific View Regional Hospital on the Pediatrics Floor for Period of Care 1. (*Note:* If you are already in the virtual hospital from a previous exercise, click on **Leave the Floor** and then on **Restart the Program** to get to the sign-in window.)
- From the Patient List, select Stephanie Brown.
- Click on **Get Report**.
- Click on **Go to Nurses' Station**.
- Click on **Chart** and then on **304**.
- Review the following sections of the chart: **Physician's Notes**, **Emergency Department**, **History and Physical**, and **Nursing Admission**.

165

1. What elements of Stephanie Brown's situation increase her risk for developing meningitis?

2. What assessment data on admissions did Stephanie Brown exhibit that would indicate a diagnosis of meningitis?

3. What additional assessments would you make? (*Hint:* Think about the pathophysiology of the disease.)

4. If Stephanie Brown were 3 months old and had this diagnosis, what other assessments could you perform?

5. Explain how each of the signs listed below is tested. Then briefly describe the response each sign would elicit in a child with meningitis.

Sign	To Test for Sign	Response in Meningitis
Nuchal rigidity		
Kernig sign		
Brudzinski sign		

6. Match each of the following physician's orders with its rationale.

Physician's Order

_____ Pulse oximetry q4h

_____ Neuro checks q4h

_____ Blood culture for fever above 101 degrees

_____ Audiogram

_____ Keep HOB elevated 45 degrees

_____ Respiratory isolation

_____ Vancomycin levels

Rationale

a. To establish baseline (aminoglycosides can cause ototoxicity)

b. To utilize gravity in reducing intracranial pressure

c. To maintain therapeutic blood level

d. To monitor neurologic status

e. To prevent transmission of disease via droplets

f. To assess for other causative agents

g. To perform ongoing monitoring of O_2 status

Exercise 2

Virtual Hospital Activity

45 minutes

- Sign in to work at Pacific View Regional Hospital on the Pediatrics Floor for Period of Care 1. (*Note:* If you are already in the virtual hospital from a previous exercise, click on **Leave the Floor** and then on **Restart the Program** to get to the sign-in window.)
- From the Patient List, select Stephanie Brown (Room 304).
- Click on **Go to Nurses' Station**.
- Click on **304** at the bottom of the screen to go to Stephanie's room.
- Click on **Patient Care**.
- Click on **Head & Neck**.
- Click on **Neurologic** in the green boxes and view the assessment.

1. State the physiologic basis for Stephanie Brown's headache. (*Hint:* Read about increased intracranial pressure in your textbook.)

- Click on **Chart** and then on **304**.
- Click on **Emergency Department** and review.
- Then, click on and read the **Nurse's Notes** and **Physician's Notes**.

2. List the clinical manifestations of meningitis exhibited by Stephanie Brown in the ED.

• Click on and read the **History and Physical** section of Stephanie Brown's chart.

3. Describe the Glasgow Coma Scale and list the three-part assessment of the coma scale.

• Click on **Laboratory Reports**. Review the findings recorded in the ED on Monday at 0100.

4. Below, list the abnormal findings you noted for Stephanie Brown in the Laboratory Reports. For each abnormal finding, give the normal range of results. Finally, what does each finding indicate?

Lab Test	Results	Normal Range	Indications

- Now click on **Diagnostic Reports** and review the summary of Stephanie Brown's lumbar puncture.

5. Below, list each of the cerebral spinal fluid (CSF) results from Stephanie Brown's lumbar puncture on Monday. For each finding, give the normal range of results and identify what each finding indicates.

CSF (Lumbar)	Results	Normal Range	Indications

- Click on **Physician's Orders** and review.

6. What medication is ordered for Stephanie Brown for a high temperature?

7. What is the rationale for administering this medication by rectum (PR) in the ED at 0100 on Monday?

8. What is the rationale for having the head of Stephanie Brown's bed elevated 45 degrees?

9. Describe the standard isolation technique for a child with meningitis in an acute care center. (*Note:* You may describe the standard practice in an institution where you work as a staff member or student.)

- Click on **Return to Nurses' Station**.
- Click on **MAR**.
- Click on tab **304** and review Stephanie Brown's records.

10. An intravenous infusion is started immediately in a child with suspected meningitis to administer IV fluids and:
    a. antiepileptic drugs.
    b. steroid drugs.
    c. blood products.
    d. antimicrobial drugs.

Now let's go to the Medication Room and prepare to administer all of the 0730 and 0800 medications ordered for Stephanie Brown.

- First, click on **Return to Nurses' Station**.
- Next, click on **Medication Room** at the bottom of the screen.
- Click on **MAR** to determine what medications Stephanie Brown should receive for 0730 and 0800. You may review the MAR at any time to verify the correct medication order. (*Hint:* Remember to look at the patient name on the MAR to make sure you have the correct record—you must click on the tab with Stephanie Brown's room number within the MAR.) Click on **Return to Medication Room** after reviewing the correct MAR.
- Click on **Unit Dosage** and then on drawer **304**.
- Select the medications you would like to administer. For each medication you select, click on **Put Medication on Tray**. When you are finished, click on **Close Drawer** at the bottom of the screen.
- Click **View Medication Room**.
- Now click on **Automated System** and **Login**.
- Select the correct patient and drawer according to the medication you want to administer. (*Hint:* This automated system is for controlled substances only.) Then click **Open Drawer**.
- Select the medication you would like to administer, click on **Put Medication on Tray**, and then click **Close Drawer**.
- Click **View Medication Room**.
- Click on **Preparation** and select the medication to administer.
- Click **Prepare** and wait for the Preparation Wizard to appear. If the Wizard requests information, provide your answer(s) and then click **Next**.
- Choose the correct patient and then click **Finish**.
- Repeat the previous three steps until all medications that you want to administer are prepared.
- You can click on **Review Your Medications** and then click through the various tabs to review the ordered and prepared medications for Stephanie Brown. When you are ready, click **Return to Medication Room**. When back in the Medication Room, go directly to Stephanie Brown's room by clicking on **304** at the bottom of the screen.

- In Stephanie Brown's room, administer the medications, utilizing the rights of medication administration. After you have collected the appropriate assessment data and are ready for administration, click **Patient Care** and then **Medication Administration**. Verify that the correct patient and medication(s) appear in the left-hand window. Then click the down arrow next to Select. From the drop-down menu, select **Administer** and complete the Administration Wizard by providing any information requested. When the Wizard stops asking for information, click **Administer to Patient**. Specify **Yes** when asked whether this administration should be recorded in the MAR. Finally, click **Finish**. Complete these steps for each medication you wish to administer.

12. In the mock MAR form below, document the medications you administered.

Medication/Dose	2300-0700	0700-1500	1500-2300

13. Stephanie Brown is receiving maintenance IV fluids with strict fluid intake and output to prevent what severe complication?

- To answer questions 14 through 16, you will need to consult the Drug Guide.
- To access the Drug Guide, click on the **Drug** icon in the lower left corner of your screen. When the Drug Guide opens, use the Search box or scroll through the list of drugs at the top of the screen; select **vancomycin**.

14. Provide the rationale for the intravenous administration of this drug (versus oral administration).

15. Briefly describe the procedure for administering vancomycin intravenously to a child Stephanie Brown's age. Include the correct dilution, if required.

16. List three serious side effects for which the nurse should be vigilant during and after the administration of this medication.

Now let's see how you did administering Stephanie Brown's medications.

- Click on **Leave the Floor** at the bottom of your screen. From the Floor Menu, select **Look at Your Preceptor's Evaluation**. Then click on **Medication Scorecard**.

- Review the scorecard to see whether or not you correctly administered the appropriate medication(s). If not, why do you think you were incorrect? According to Table C in this scorecard, what resources should be used and what important assessments should be completed before administering the medication(s)? Did you utilize these resources and perform these assessments correctly?

- Print a copy of the Medication Scorecard for your instructor to evaluate.

- Click on **Return to Evaluations**.

- Click on **Return to Menu**.

Care of the Child with Cerebral Palsy

Reading Assignments:

McKinney, James, Murray, Nelson, and Ashwill: Maternal-Child Nursing, 5th edition
(Chapters 7 and 52)

Perry, Hockenberry, Lowdermilk, and Wilson: Maternal Child Nursing Care, 5th edition
(Chapters 38 and 49)

Patient: Stephanie Brown, Room 304

Objectives:

- Describe the behaviors and problems associated with the most common types of cerebral palsy (CP).
- Discuss a range of etiologic factors associated with CP.
- Explain the importance of early diagnosis and treatment to the child's optimal level of function.
- Discuss the nursing care needs of a child with CP.

Exercise 1

Virtual Hospital Activity

30 minutes

- Sign in to work at Pacific View Regional Hospital on the Pediatrics Floor for Period of Care 1. (*Note:* If you are already in the virtual hospital from a previous exercise, click on **Leave the Floor** and then on **Restart the Program** to get to the sign-in window.)
- From the Patient List, select Stephanie Brown.
- Click on **Get Report**.
- Click on **Go to Nurses' Station**.

1. What is cerebral palsy (CP)?

- Click on **Chart** and then on **304**.
- Click on and review the **History and Physical**.
- Click on **Return to Nurses' Station**.
- Click on **304** to go to Stephanie Brown's room.
- Click on **Patient Care** and then on **Physical Assessment**. Perform a focused assessment.

2. Based on your assessment of Stephanie Brown, list any behaviors she demonstrates that are associated with CP.

3. What might be an etiologic factor in Stephanie Brown's situation?

4. Early recognition and treatment are important to fostering achievement of optimal development. Why is CP often not diagnosed until about 2 years of age?

• Click on **Nurse-Client Interactions**.
• Select and view the video titled **0750: Caring for the Child with CP**. (*Note*: Check the virtual clock to see whether enough time has elapsed. You can use the fast-forward feature to advance the time by 2-minute intervals if the video is not yet available. Then click again on **Patient Care** and **Nurse-Client Interactions** to refresh the screen.)

5. What is the nurse doing as she listens to Stephanie Brown's mother explain problems Stephanie has related to CP.

6. What problem is Stephanie Brown at risk for during her hospitalization? (*Hint:* You will need to consider her developmental age.)

- Click on **Chart** and then on **304**.
- Click on **Nursing Admission** and review for data about Stephanie's development.

7. Assume Stephanie Brown has recently turned 3 years of age. Using the information in your textbook regarding milestones for her age, determine one skill that Stephanie should have completed, one that she is working on, and one that she is not yet ready for. Do this for one of the four skill areas (gross motor, language, cognitive, fine motor, and personal/social).

Exercise 2

Virtual Hospital Activity

20 minutes

- Sign in to work at Pacific View Regional Hospital on the Pediatrics Floor for Period of Care 3. (*Note:* If you are already in the virtual hospital from a previous exercise, click on **Leave the Floor** and then on **Restart the Program** to get to the sign-in window.)
- From the Patient List, select Stephanie Brown.
- Click on **Get Report**.
- Click on **Go to Nurses' Station**.
- Click on **Chart** and then on **304**.
- Review Stephanie's records, in particular her **History and Physical**.

1. What type of CP does Stephanie Brown have? What are the signs that she manifests?

2. Match each type of CP with its description.

Type	Description
_____ Spastic	a. Rigid flexor and extensor muscles; tremors
_____ Dyskinetic/athetoid	b. Increased deep tendon reflexes, hypertonia, flexion, and scissors gait
_____ Ataxic	c. Slow, writhing uncontrolled and involuntary movements
_____ Rigid	d. Loss of coordination, equilibrium, and kinesthetic sense

3. What are some aspects of a child's life on which CP can have an impact? Make sure that at least one of your answers is a psychosocial concern.

- Click on **Return to Nurses' Station**.
- Click on **304**.
- Click on **Patient Care** and then on **Nurse-Client Interactions**.
- Select and view the video titled **1530: Preventive Measures**. (*Note*: Check the virtual clock to see whether enough time has elapsed. You can use the fast-forward feature to advance the time by 2-minute intervals if the video is not yet available. Then click again on **Patient Care** and **Nurse-Client Interactions** to refresh the screen.)

4. Why does Stephanie Brown require heel cord stretching?

5. What other preventive measures have been integrated into Stephanie Brown's regimen to prevent complications associated with CP?

6. What is the nursing role with regard to supporting these endeavors?

7. Explain why nutrition is so important for the child who has CP.

Exercise 3

Writing Activity

15 minutes

1. Develop a plan to teach Stephanie Brown's mother to promote self-esteem as Stephanie progresses through the stage of initiative versus guilt. First, write one or more goals.

2. Now develop nursing interventions designed to meet the goal(s) you wrote in question 1.

3. What does your community offer for children with special care needs?

4. What other local or state resources are available for these types of needs? Please include resources that would meet the needs of a wide variety of ages.

Care of the Child with Anorexia

Reading Assignments:

McKinney, James, Murray, Nelson, and Ashwill: Maternal-Child Nursing, 5th edition
   (Chapters 9 and 53)
Perry, Hockenberry, Lowdermilk, and Wilson: Maternal Child Nursing Care, 5th edition
   (Chapters 29 and 35)

Patient: Tiffany Sheldon, Room 305

Objectives:

- Compare and contrast the description, etiology, and typical behaviors associated with anorexia nervosa and bulimia nervosa.
- Discuss the physiologic impact of anorexia nervosa and bulimia nervosa.
- Discuss the multidisciplinary approach necessary for treatment of eating disorders.
- Explore the challenges of providing nursing care for patients with anorexia nervosa or bulimia nervosa.

Exercise 1

Writing Activity

15 minutes

1. Compare and contrast anorexia and bulimia by matching each problem with its characteristics. (*Hint:* Although some behaviors may seem to overlap, they are usually associated more closely with one problem rather than the other. Choose the problem *most* closely associated with each characteristic.)

Characteristic	**Problem**
_____ Deliberate refusal of food to maintain body weight	a. Anorexia nervosa
_____ Recurrent episodes of binging and a sense of loss of control	b. Bulimia nervosa
_____ Excessive use of vomiting, laxatives, diuretics, or exercise	
_____ Possible amenorrhea—both primary and secondary	
_____ Persistent irrational concern with body weight and shape	
_____ Body image that is contrary to reality	
_____ Ritualistic eating pattern	
_____ Binge eating and purging	
_____ Muscle wasting, dull and brittle hair, lanugo	
_____ Risk for fluid and electrolyte imbalance	
_____ Tooth erosion	

2. Give an example of an eating pattern that might be found in a person with anorexia nervosa. What often underlies such behavior?

3. How is it believed that family function and culture play into the problem of eating disorders?

4. What are some secondary gains achieved through eating disorders? (*Hint:* Secondary gains are indirect "benefits" that the patient gets from having his or her disease.)

Exercise 2

Virtual Hospital Activity

30 minutes

- Sign in to work at Pacific View Regional Hospital on the Pediatrics Floor for Period of Care 1. (*Note:* If you are already in the virtual hospital from a previous exercise, click on **Leave the Floor** and then on **Restart the Program** to get to the sign-in window.)
- From the Patient List, select Tiffany Sheldon.
- Click on **Go to Nurses' Station**.
- Click on **Chart** and then on **305**.
- Review the **Nursing Admission** and the **History and Physical**.

1. What in Tiffany Sheldon's history is indicative of her diagnosis of anorexia nervosa?

2. Did you identify the family crisis (divorce of parents) as a precipitating factor in Tiffany Sheldon's situation? Did you include the fact that she is an "A" student in your list? Why should you see these factors as red flags?

- Click on **Return to Nurses' Station**.
- Click on **305** at the bottom of the screen.
- Click on **Patient Care**.
- Complete a head-to-toe assessment, watching for assessment data that are consistent with anorexia nervosa.

3. As you complete your assessment, what stands out to you? How much does nutritional status affect the total patient?

- Click on **Nurse-Client Interactions**.
- Select and view the video titled **0730: Initial Assessment**. (*Note*: Check the virtual clock to see whether enough time has elapsed. You can use the fast-forward feature to advance the time by 2-minute intervals if the video is not yet available. Then click again on **Patient Care** and **Nurse-Client Interactions** to refresh the screen.)

4. Tiffany Sheldon has been described as having a flat affect, being withdrawn, and avoiding eye contact. How would you describe her behavior at the time of this interaction?

5. What is the most effective communication to use with Tiffany Sheldon?

6. In addition to nursing assessment, what multidimensional assessments and interventions are important to developing an appropriate plan of care for Tiffany?

7. How do you think Tiffany Sheldon might respond to being told that she will be seen by an Eating Disorders Team?

8. What is the nurse's role in identifying and/or coordinating care and services that Tiffany Sheldon requires during her inpatient stay?

Exercise 3

Virtual Hospital Activity

45 minutes

The first order of business with a patient who has anorexia nervosa is to correct any imbalances. Keep this in mind as you work through this exercise.

- Sign in to work at Pacific View Regional Hospital on the Pediatrics Floor for Period of Care 1. (*Note:* If you are already in the virtual hospital from a previous exercise, click on **Leave the Floor** and then on **Restart the Program** to get to the sign-in window.)
- From the Patient List, select Tiffany Sheldon.
- Click on **Go to Nurses' Station**.
- Click on **Chart** and then on **305**.
- Review the chart, especially the **Physician's Orders** and the **Laboratory Reports**.

1. What is being done to assess for and manage Tiffany Sheldon's fluid and electrolyte imbalance?

2. What do Tiffany Sheldon's lab results tell you about her fluid and electrolyte status? Report on the ones that give you specific information.

3. Tiffany Sheldon did not have a pH level done. A patient with anorexia nervosa is at risk for metabolic alkalosis. What would happen to the pH in this instance?

4. List the objective assessment data that indicate Tiffany Sheldon is dehydrated.

5. Why is Tiffany Sheldon on a cardiac monitor?

6. Tiffany Sheldon is receiving IV fluid with potassium chloride added. What is the order? What are the nursing responsibilities before and during potassium administration?

7. a. Identify a generic nursing diagnosis for hydration problems in patients with anorexia nervosa.

   b. Now rewrite this nursing diagnosis so that it accurately reflects Tiffany's situation.

Next, begin thinking about how adequate caloric intake is achieved.

- Click on **Return to Nurse's Station** and then on **Leave the Floor**.
- From the Floor Menu, select **Restart the Program**.
- Sign in to work at Pacific View Regional Hospital on the Pediatrics Floor for Period of Care 2.
- From the Patient List, select Tiffany Sheldon.
- Click on **Go to Nurses' Station** and then on **305** at the bottom of the screen.
- Click on **Patient Care** and then on **Nurse-Client Interactions**.
- Select and view the video titled **1115: Managing Anorexia Nervosa**. (*Note*: Check the virtual clock to see whether enough time has elapsed. You can use the fast-forward feature to advance the time by 2-minute intervals if the video is not yet available. Then click again on **Patient Care** and **Nurse-Client Interactions** to refresh the screen.)

8. Discuss the cultural beliefs and personal perceptions that influence the development of eating disorders. Consider both males and females in your discussion.

9. What is the value of an eating (behavior) contract for Tiffany Sheldon?

10. What is the rationale for the diet orders that are part of the eating (behavior) contract?

11. The eating contract specifies _____ calories per day to facilitate weight gain.

12. What supportive interventions might the nurse provide to help Tiffany Sheldon remain compliant?

Now, consider the emotional aspects of Tiffany Sheldon's care.

- Click on **Leave the Floor** and then on **Restart the Program**.
- Sign in to work at Pacific View Regional Hospital on the Pediatrics Floor for Period of Care 3.
- From the Patient List, select Tiffany Sheldon.
- Click on **Go to Nurses' Station**.
- Click on **305** at the bottom of the screen.
- Click on **Patient Care** and then on **Nurse-Client Interactions**.
- Select and view the video titled **1500: Relapse—Contributing Factors**. (*Note*: Check the virtual clock to see whether enough time has elapsed. You can use the fast-forward feature to advance the time by 2-minute intervals if the video is not yet available. Then click again on **Patient Care** and **Nurse-Client Interactions** to refresh the screen.)

13. What does Tiffany Sheldon say about what has caused her relapse? What recent events, if any, may have contributed to her having an acute episode of her anorexia nervosa?

14. What did the psychiatrist do to effectively elicit Tiffany Sheldon's concerns?

15. What multidimensional factors will contribute to Tiffany Sheldon's ability to comply with the eating contract that has been developed? What barriers may be present?

16. A patient with an eating disorder may not like the sensations associated with refeeding. Develop strategies to help Tiffany Sheldon overcome barriers to the success of her eating disorder plan.

17. School nurses or nurses in community settings may play several roles with teens who have anorexia nervosa. Discuss one of the primary roles.

Care of the Hospitalized Child

Reading Assignments:

McKinney, James, Murray, Nelson, and Ashwill: Maternal-Child Nursing, 5th edition
(Chapters 39, 43, 52, and 54)

Perry, Hockenberry, Lowdermilk, and Wilson: Maternal Child Nursing Care, 5th edition
(Chapters 30, 41, and 45)

Patient: Stephanie Brown, Room 304

Objectives:

- Describe the nursing care of the child with meningitis and constipation.
- Identify the rationale for auditory testing in the child with meningitis.

Exercise 1

Virtual Hospital Activity

45 minutes

- Sign in to work at Pacific View Regional Hospital on the Pediatrics Floor for Period of Care 2. (*Note:* If you are already in the virtual hospital from a previous exercise, click on **Leave the Floor** and then **Restart the Program** to get to the sign-in window.)
- From the Patient List, select Stephanie Brown (Room 304).
- Click on **Go to Nurses' Station**.
- Click on **Chart** and then on **304**.
- Click on **Emergency Department** and review this report.
- Click on and review the **Physician's Orders** and **Physician's Notes** for Wednesday at 0900.
- Click on **Return to Nurses' Station**.
- Click on **304** at the bottom of the screen to go to Stephanie Brown's room.
- Click **Patient Care** and then **Nurse-Client Interactions**.
- Select and view the video titled **1120: Preventing Spread of Disease**. (*Note:* Check the virtual clock to see whether enough time has elapsed. You can use the fast-forward feature to advance the time by 2-minute intervals if the video is not yet available. Then click on **Patient Care** and **Nurse-Client Interactions** to refresh the screen.)

1. What might explain why the physician decreased Stephanie Brown's IV rate to 10 mL/hr?

2. How did Stephanie Brown's nurse explain the basis for the respiratory isolation?

3. Based on your earlier review of the Physician's Notes, what was the physician's most likely rationale for discontinuing the respiratory isolation and vancomycin for Stephanie Brown?

• Still in Stephanie Brown's room, click on **Clinical Alerts** and review.

4. What does the Clinical Alert say regarding Stephanie Brown's abdominal assessment?

5. When did Stephanie Brown have her last bowel movement?

- Click on **Chart** and then **304**.
- Review the **Physician's Notes** to answer question 6.

6. Compare the Monday and Wednesday notes in regard to the Kernig sign, Brudzinski sign, and nuchal rigidity results for Stephanie Brown. Record any changes below. (*Hint:* See the relevant section in your textbook.)

- Click on **Return to Room 304**.
- Click on **MAR** and then on tab **304** to review Stephanie Brown's medication orders.

7. Are there further indications for performing an audiogram (hearing test) on this patient (besides the diagnosis of meningitis)?

- Click on **Return to Room 304**.
- Click on **Chart** and then on **304**.
- Click on **Physician's Orders** and review the orders for 1100 on Wednesday.

8. What medication is ordered for Stephanie Brown at this time?

- Click on **Return to Room 304**.
- Click on the **Drug** icon in the lower left corner of your screen.

9. Complete the following table for the drug you identified in question 8. Relate your answers specifically to Stephanie Brown's need for the medication.

Name of Medication	Classification	Action	Dosage	Frequency	Route

- Click on **Return to Room 304**.
- Click on **Medication Room** at the bottom of the screen.
- Click on **Unit Dosage** and then on **Drawer 304**.
- Select the medication that you would like to administer and click **Put Medication on Tray**. Click **Close Drawer** at the bottom of the screen and then click **View Medication Room**.
- Click on **Preparation** and then click **Prepare** next to the medication you identified in question 8.
- When you have finished the steps of the Preparation Wizard, click on **Return to Medication Room** and then on **304** at the bottom of the screen to go to Stephanie Brown's room.
- Administer the medication, utilizing the rights of medication administration. After you have collected the appropriate assessment data and are ready for administration, click **Patient Care** and then **Medication Administration**. Verify that the correct patient and medication(s) appear in the left-hand window. Then click the down arrow next to Select. From the drop-down menu, select **Administer** and complete the Administration Wizard by providing any information requested. When the Wizard stops asking for information, click **Administer to Patient**. Specify **Yes** when asked whether this administration should be recorded in the MAR. Finally, click **Finish**.

10. On the mock MAR below, document the medication you just administered to Stephanie Brown. Indicate the time you gave it in the correct column.

Medication/Dose	2300-0700	0700-1500	1500-2300

Now let's see how you did!

- Click on **Leave the Floor** at the bottom of your screen. From the Floor Menu, select **Look at Your Preceptor's Evaluation**. Then click on **Medication Scorecard**.
- Review the scorecard to see whether or not you correctly administered the appropriate medication. If not, why do you think you were incorrect? According to Table C in this scorecard, what resources should be used and what important assessments should be completed before administering the medication(s)? Did you utilize these resources and perform these assessments correctly?
- Print a copy of the Medication Scorecard for your instructor to evaluate.
- Click **Return to Evaluations**.
- Click **Return to Menu**.

In your textbook, read about behavioral measures and physiologic measures.

- Click **Return to Evaluations** and then **Return to Menu**.
- Click **Restart the Program** and sign in to work on the Pediatrics Floor for Period of Care 2.
- From the Patient List, select Stephanie Brown (Room 304).
- Click on **Go to Nurses' Station**.
- Click on **EPR** and then on **Login**.
- Select **304** from the Patient drop-down menu as the patient's room and **Vital Signs** from the Category drop-down menu as the category.

11. Compare Stephanie Brown's blood pressure and pain scale rating on Wednesday 0700 with her BP and pain rating on Wednesday at 1100.

12. Using the FACES pain rating scale below, place an X on the face that matches Stephanie Brown's description of her headache recorded on Wednesday at 1100.

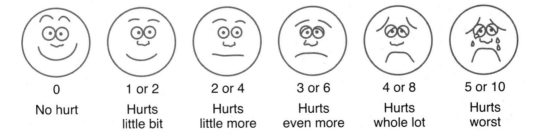

0	1 or 2	2 or 4	3 or 6	4 or 8	5 or 10
No hurt	Hurts little bit	Hurts little more	Hurts even more	Hurts whole lot	Hurts worst

- Click on **Exit EPR**.
- Click on **Chart** and then on **304**.
- Once again, review the **Physician's Orders** for Stephanie Brown.

13. What is ordered that can be administered to alleviate her headache?

- Click on **Return to Nurses' Station**.
- Now click on the **Drug** icon in the lower left corner of your screen.

14. Using the Drug Guide as your reference, complete the following table for the medication you identified in question 13.

Name of Medication	Classification	Action	Dose	Frequency	Route

- Click on **Chart** and then on **304**.
- Review the **Nurse's Notes** for Tuesday at 2300 and Wednesday at 0600.

15. Based on your assessment of Stephanie Brown at this time, what route would be appropriate for administering the medication you identified in question 13? State your rationale for choosing this route.

Care of the Child with a Head Injury

Reading Assignments:

McKinney, James, Murray, Nelson, and Ashwill: Maternal-Child Nursing, 5th edition
(Chapters 34 and 52)

Perry, Hockenberry, Lowdermilk, and Wilson: Maternal Child Nursing Care, 5th edition
(Chapters 38 and 45)

Patient: Tommy Douglas, Room 302

Objectives:

- Evaluate the pathophysiology related to acute head trauma in children.
- Participate in the care of a comatose child.
- Review medications given to a child who has experienced a head injury.
- Identify factors that culminate in a stressful environment in the Emergency Department.
- Discuss nursing interventions supportive to the child and family who are in the Emergency Department.

Exercise 1

Virtual Hospital Activity

20 minutes

- Sign in to work at Pacific View Regional Hospital on the Pediatrics Floor for Period of Care 1. (*Note:* If you are already in the virtual hospital from a previous exercise, click on **Leave the Floor** and then **Restart the Program** to get to the sign-in window.)
- From the Patient List, select Tommy Douglas (Room 302).
- Click on **Go to Nurses' Station**.
- Click on **Chart** and then on **302**.
- Click on and review the **Nursing Admission**.

1. What are the clinical symptoms of increased intracranial pressure (ICP) in a child Tommy Douglas' age and in his current condition?

2. What is the definition of increased ICP?

3. List three causes of increased ICP.

4. Why is the concern for increased ICP important when caring for a patient with a head injury?

5. Which of the following vital sign changes are associated with brainstem injury following acute head trauma? Select all that apply.

_____ Rapid or intermittent respirations

_____ Wide fluctuations in pulse

_____ Widening pulse pressure

_____ Extreme fluctuations in blood pressure

_____ Elevated temperature

6. Explain what is meant by blunt trauma.

7. Explain the mechanism of the acceleration-deceleration injury that occurs with a major head injury.

8. What are the priorities for initial management of a head injury?

Exercise 2

Virtual Hospital Activity

25 minutes

- Sign in to work at Pacific View Regional Hospital on the Pediatrics Floor for Period of Care 1. (*Note:* If you are already in the virtual hospital from a previous exercise, click on **Leave the Floor** and then on **Restart the Program** to get to the sign-in window.)
- From the Patient List, select Tommy Douglas (Room 302).
- Click on **Go to Nurses' Station**.
- Click on **Chart** and then on **302**.
- Select the **Emergency Department** tab and review the ED admission notes.
- While in the chart, also click on and review the **Nurse's Notes** and the **History and Physical.**

1. What caused Tommy Douglas' head injury?

- Now click on **Expired MARs** and review Tommy Douglas' expired MAR for Sunday at 2300.
- Next, click on **Physician's Orders** and review orders written in the ED.
- For additional help with the following questions, consult the Drug Guide by first clicking on **Return to Nurses' Station** and then clicking either on the **Drug** icon in the lower left corner of the screen or on the **Drug Guide** itself on the counter.

2. Based on your knowledge of head injury, why did Tommy Douglas receive mannitol?

3. Describe the sequence of events from Tommy Douglas' admission to the Emergency Department to his admission to your unit. (*Hint:* For help, check the Nurse's Notes, Physician's Notes, and Physician's Orders sections of the chart.)

4. List three interventions specific to the treatment of a child with a head injury that were performed before Tommy Douglas' arrival on your unit.

Exercise 3

Virtual Hospital Activity

35 minutes

- Sign in to work at Pacific View Regional Hospital on the Pediatrics Floor for Period of Care 1. (*Note:* If you are already in the virtual hospital from a previous exercise, click on **Leave the Floor** and then on **Restart the Program** to get to the sign-in window.)
- From the Patient List, select Tommy Douglas (Room 302).
- Click on **Go to Nurses' Station**.
- Click on **Chart** and then on **302** to access Tommy's chart.
- Click on **Emergency Department** and review the admission notes.
- Click on and review the **Nurse's Notes** and the **Physician's Notes**.

1. What are the three major components of the Glasgow Coma Scale?

Now let's assess Tommy Douglas' neurologic status over time since his admission to the ED. To do this, access and find neurologic assessment data in the following resources, recording your findings in the table as instructed in question 2.

- In the patient's chart, click on **Emergency Department** and review this report for Sunday admission.
- Next, click on **Physician's Notes** and review the notes for Monday 0930 and Tuesday 1730.
- Click on **Return to Nurses' Station**.
- Select **EPR** and click on **Login**.
- Specify **302** as the room number and **Neurologic** as the category.
- Review the neurologic findings for 0715 Wednesday.

2. In the table below, record the findings from your chart review of Tommy Douglas' neurologic status on Sunday, Monday, Tuesday, and Wednesday.

Neurologic Exam	Sunday Admission	Monday 0930	Tuesday 1730	Wednesday 0715
GCS: Total Score				
Pupils Right: Size				
Pupils Right: Reaction				
Pupils Left: Size				
Pupils Left: Reaction				
Cranial Nerves I-XII				
Orientation				
Perception and Cognition				
Mental Status				
Sensory				

- Click on **Exit EPR**.
- From the Nurses' Station click on **Leave the Floor**.
- At the Floor Menu, select **Restart the Program**.
- Sign in to work on the Pediatrics Floor for Period of Care 2.
- Again, select Tommy Douglas (Room 302) as your patient and click on **Go to Nurses' Station**.
- Now click on **EPR** and then on **Login**.
- Choose **302** as the patient's room and **Neurologic** as the category. Review the results of the neurologic assessment recorded on Wednesday at 0800.

3.

NEUROLOGIC ASSESSMENT				
Pupils	Right	Size		
		Reaction		
	Left	Size		
		Reaction		

++ = Brisk
+ = Sluggish
− = No reaction
C = Eye closed by swelling

Pupil scale (mm): 1, 2, 3, 4, 5, 6, 7, 8

GLASGOW COMA SCALE

Eyes open	Spontaneously	4	
	To speech	3	
	To pain	2	
	None	1	

Best motor response	Obeys commands	6	
	Localizes pain	5	
	Flexion withdrawal	4	
	Flexion abnormal	3	
	Extension	2	
	None	1	

Usually record best arm or age-appropriate response

Best response to auditory and/or visual stimulus	>2 years		<2 years
	Orientation	5	5 Smiles, listens, follows
	Confused	4	4 Cries, consolable
	Inappropriate words	3	3 Inappropriate persistent cry
	Incomprehensible words	2	2 Agitated, restless
	None	1	1 No response
	Endotracheal tube or trach	T	

COMA SCALE TOTAL	

HAND GRIP:
Equal
Unequal
R____L
Weakness

LOC:
Alert/oriented x4
Sleepy
Irritable
Comatose
Disoriented
Combative
Lethargic
Awake
Sleeping
Drowsy
Agitated

MUSCLE TONE:
Normal
Arching
Spastic
Flaccid
Weak
Decorticate
Decerebrate
Other _____

EYE MOVEMENT:
Normal
Nystagmus
Strabismus
Other _____

FONTANEL/ WINDOW:
Soft
Flat
Sunken
Tense
Bulging
Closed
Other _____

MOOD/AFFECT:
Happy
Content
Quiet
Withdrawn
Sad
Flat
Hostile

Complete the Glasgow Coma Scale readings below, using the findings from Tommy Douglas' neurologic examination at 0800 Wednesday morning.

Pupils right: size: _____

Pupils right: reaction: _____

Pupils left: size: _____

Pupils left: reaction: _____

Eyes open: _____

Best motor response: _____

Best response to auditory and or visual stimulus: _____

Endotracheal tube or trach: _____

Coma Scale total: _____

Hand grip: _____

LOC: _____

Muscle tone: _____

Eye movement: _____

Fontanel/window: _____

Mood/affect: _____

4. How did Tommy Douglas' neurologic assessment results change from early in his admission to the PICU (Monday) to his admission to the telemetry unit (Wednesday)? Document your findings below. (*Hint:* Go to the chart and review the Nurse's Notes and Physician's Notes.)

Monday

Wednesday

5. List the following activities in order of priority beginning with what you would assess first when examining a critically ill patient such as Tommy Douglas.

_____ Check intravenous fluids and lines

_____ Perform a physical assessment

_____ Check ventilator settings

_____ Obtain vital signs

Exercise 4

Writing Activity

20 minutes

1. List and explain five or six factors that can contribute to creating a stressful environment when a child is brought to the Emergency Department after a traumatic event.

2. For each of the factors you listed above, develop a nursing intervention to minimize stress. If you have had experience in such an environment (even during an observation), you have an opportunity to be creative here.

3. Choose two age groups of children that you would find especially challenging to work with in the Emergency Department. For each age group, explain the challenges and share a nursing intervention to help. Parents and caregivers need a great deal of support. Nurses need to be able to anticipate fears and anxieties in order to craft careful communication to elicit and respond to concerns.

4. What are the three greatest fears parents have when their child is brought to the Emergency Department?

5. Parents may feel pushed aside in the Emergency Department. How can the nurse deal with this problem?

Notes:

Notes:

Notes:

Notes: